LEARNING AND REINFORCEMENT

Stephen Walker

Methuen

To Lynne and Becky

First published in 1975 by Methuen & Co Ltd
11 New Fetter Lane, London EC4P 4EE
© 1975 Stephen Walker
Printed in Great Britain by
Richard Clay (The Chaucer Press), Ltd
Bungay, Suffolk

ISBN (hardback) 0 416 82780 2
ISBN (paperback) 0 416 82790 X

We are grateful to Grant McIntyre of
Open Books Publishing Ltd
for assistance in the preparation of this series

Contents

Editor's Introduction

One very important strand in the psychological tradition is the view of man as a biological organism. His functional interaction with his environment has been the focus of the studies of learning which Stephen Walker reviews in this book. He also indicates in the course of his account several of the ways in which this theoretical approach has been applied to human problems. Finally, he discusses the extent to which it is possible to use learning theory to explain complex human behaviour.

What unifies Unit A of *Essential Psychology* is the notion of the human being as a processor of information. Like a computer we can register information, code it, perform operations on the coded version, store the result, and subsequently retrieve it. Moreover, like a computer, we can use our output, or behaviour, as feedback or evidence by which to monitor our subsequent performance. The authors in Unit A are more concerned with making generalizations about people than with exploring their individual differences. Further, they deal with personal mental processes rather than with interpersonal social processes. They also probably place more stress on the traditional scientific experiments as a source of evidence than do most of the authors of the other units.

The computer analogy is very useful for handling the sort of evidence we get from experiments. For most experiments provide the experimental subject with input or information through the senses and then subsequently measure behaviour, or output; they then make inferences about the processes which occur between the two observable events. However, the computer analogy may not be suitable for handling other situations, where there is no immediate sensory experience or no easily definable consequent behaviour. And some psychologists also feel that it detracts from the concept of the individual as a person who can consciously act upon and control his environment. The reader will find other general conceptual frameworks in other units. Psychology is struggling to do justice to the complexities of its subject matter; it is hardly likely to find any single analogy to encompass the richness of human behaviour and experience. Coming to terms with a variety of explanatory frameworks decreases our confidence in psychology as a mature science; but perhaps it is best that we should be honest about what we don't know.

Essential Psychology as a whole is designed to reflect this changing structure and function of psychology. The authors are both academics and professionals, and their aim has been to introduce the most important concepts in their areas to beginning students. They have tried to do so clearly, but have not attempted to conceal the fact that concepts that now appear central to their work may soon be peripheral. In other words, they have presented psychology as a developing set of views of man, not as a body of received truth. Readers are not intended to study the whole series in order to 'master the basics'. Rather, since different people may wish to use different theoretical frameworks for their own purposes, the series has been designed so that each title stands on its own. But it is possible that if the reader has read no psychology before, he will enjoy individual books more if he has read the introductions (A1, B1 etc.) to the units to which they belong. Readers of the units concerned with applications of psychology (E, F) may benefit from reading all the introductions.

A word about references in the text to the work of other writers – e.g. 'Smith 1974'. These occur where the author feels he must acknowledge an important concept or some crucial evidence by name. The book or article referred to will be listed in the bibliography (which doubles as name index) at the back of the book. The reader is invited to consult these sources if he wishes to explore topics further. A list of general further reading is also to be found at the back of the book.

We hope you enjoy psychology.

Peter Herriot

I
Introduction

In 1866 the St Petersburg Censorial Committee banned a popular book, and prosecuted its author for undermining public morals. The author was not a political theorist, or a pornographer, but a physiologist called Sechenov. The book, *Reflexes of the Brain*, introduced the controversial suggestion that 'all acts of conscious or unconscious life are reflexes'. This assertion seemed to over-simplify human existence by reducing thought and action to mechanical processes. However, the Censorial Committee's view that public morals would suffer because of this oversimplification was not supported by the courts, and the case against Sechenov collapsed.

A few years later, in London, *The Times* was concerned that 'morality would lose all elements of stable authority' if the public were to believe the ideas expressed in another controversial book, Darwin's *The Descent of Man*. But in the next decade Darwin was buried in Westminster Abbey, with *The Times'* full approval.

The two ideas which initially angered the critics of Sechenov and Darwin are central to the field of 'learning and reinforcement' in psychology. The first idea is that human acts and thoughts can be interpreted as reflexes, or learned responses, and the second that human psychology is closely connected to animal psychology. Despite the recognition eventually given to Sechenov and Darwin there is still today considerable unease about this approach to human psychology. It is judged as immoral, or ineffective, and often as both. It is certainly ineffective in the sense that doing laboratory experiments in the search for psychological principles is a very indirect way of finding out about particularly human activities. For instance, in the psychology of industry or advertising, direct specialized information based on experience might be a much more effective source of knowledge about these activities (and can be found in unit E of *Essential Psychology*). However, if there are any general principles which underlie human and animal behaviour, then knowledge of them might very well add something to our capacity for understanding and changing human behaviour in a wide variety of contexts. In fact during the last twenty years, considerable advances have been made in the application of general psychological principles in the areas of education and mental illness.

To the extent that such applications work, it is sometimes felt that it is immoral to use them, because psychologists ought not to use their knowledge to manipulate others. Whereas *The Times* was concerned in 1871 lest the publication of Darwin's book should spread the revolution of the Paris Commune to England, critics of B. F. Skinner, who is in some ways the Sechenov of the present day, seem to fear totalitarian manipulation along the lines of Aldous Huxley's *Brave New World*. It is wise to take account of such forebodings, but it may be that new theories which apparently demystify and belittle the human psyche are strange and threatening, and become identified with other threatening issues without much justification. The aim of this book is to allow readers to become more familiar with the work of Skinner, and other theories in the tradition of Sechenov and Darwin, so that they may make their own judgements about whether such investigations pose threats, or whether they offer a useful basis for a deeper understanding of human problems with more successful design of practical solutions. In this chapter I will give a brief account of how the current concepts of *learning* and *reinforcement* have been developed.

Development of the concepts of learning and reinforcement

Darwin

Darwin had little to say about learning itself. However, he discussed many issues that are related to learning, because he was deeply concerned with differences between man and animals. To support the revolutionary belief that man is a species which has gradually evolved from an ape-like ancestor, Darwin devoted two chapters of his book *The Descent of Man* (the book which outraged *The Times* in 1871) to evidence which had convinced him that all of the 'mental powers' characteristic of man were possessed in a humbler form by lower animals. Because Darwin made rather wild inferences from casual observations of animals, he went further in the direction of over-estimating their abilities than would be justified by modern experimental methods. He attributed to various animals not only 'attention', 'imagination', 'reason' and 'abstraction' but primitive forms of the 'sense of beauty', 'belief in God' and 'moral sense'. 'Although these terms now sound far-fetched, much of the observational data Darwin quoted has remained fresh; for example, tool-using by apes and the use of informative warning signals by birds are current research topics.

While acknowledging the 'immense' superiority of human mental powers, Darwin was satisfied that they were not 'fundamentally' different from those possessed by other animals, and thus presented no barrier to his theory of evolution. For instance, man's ability to use language was solely due to his 'almost infinitely larger power of associating together the most diversified sounds and ideas' (Darwin, 1871, p. 131). So, by firmly connecting human with animal mental capacities, and by identifying the power of association as a critical factor in human intelligence, Darwin prepared the ground for 'associationist' theories about psychology, such as Pavlov's, which derived their supporting evidence from experiments with animals.

Pavlov and the conditioned reflex

The work of Pavlov has been influential in a number of ways, but the aspect of his work which stands out most clearly in comparison with Darwin's speculation, is his rigorous application of scientific method. Darwin frequently discussed the behaviour of dogs, but his method involved only the imaginative interpretation of a casual observation, often of his own pets. For instance, Darwin was prepared to attribute abstract thought to dogs on the basis of a game played with his terrier: Darwin would say 'Hi, hi, where is it?' in an eager tone, and the terrier would rush around, apparently hunting. 'Now do not these actions clearly show that she had in her mind a general idea or

11

concept that some animal is to be discovered or hunted?' asked Darwin. The answer is no. There are any number of other possibilities. The eagerness of Darwin's voice may simply have excited her. Darwin's attention or attitude may have encouraged (and 'reinforced') her hunting responses. There is just no way to deduce an explanation of the dog's behaviour from the casual observation.

Pavlov provided observations that were the opposite of casual. Dogs were placed in a separate room from the observer. The most scrupulous care was taken to avoid extraneous influences by such measures as using double walls filled with sand for sound insulation. Above all, a quantitative and completely unambiguous index was used to measure the outcome of experiments: the number of drops of saliva which the dog secreted. How did Pavlov come to choose this unlikely-sounding index? In fact, by not choosing it at all, but by making an accidental discovery. As Alexander Fleming is said to have done in his discovery of penicillin, Pavlov paid full attention to an unexpected result. He was studying salivation from the point of view of a professor of physiology who had already been awarded the Nobel prize in his special field of digestive secretions. There was an unexpected finding – that dogs often salivated when there seemed no physiological reason for them to do so. Pavlov realized that these were 'psychological secretions' and went on to make a systematic experimental analysis of exactly what psychological factors were needed to produce the salivation. As we shall discuss in Chapter 3, the main factor is that the dog learns an association between food and a signal for food. Thus if a bell is always rung just before a dog is given food, the dog salivates when he hears the bell, and we have Pavlov's well-known 'conditioned reflex'. The laboratory findings with the reflex of salivation were taken as a model for a wide range of psychological functions: 'It is obvious that the different kinds of habits based on training, education and discipline of any sort are nothing but a long chain of conditioned reflexes' (Pavlov, 1927, p. 395). Here is an echo of Sechenov's slogan 'all acts are reflexes', and although Pavlov was not taught by him, Pavlov's work seems to put into practice Sechenov's recommendation of studying psychology via reflexes.

Watson and behaviourism

The suggestion that psychologists should ignore inner feelings and thoughts was first made by J. B. Watson in 1913. Watson's initial interest was in animal psychology, and he was concerned by the difficulty of applying the methods used by his colleagues working with people. Their methods were based on self-analysis ('introspection') by either the psychologist or his subjects. Even if animals are capable of introspection, it is very difficult to be certain about what their feelings and thoughts are (but see Ch. 9). However, one can be reasonably sure about what animals are *doing*, if their behaviour is described in an objective and reliable way. Watson found that some of the questions he was concerned with, such as whether animals see colours, could be answered much more effectively if the issue of the animal's subjective sensations was ignored. For instance, it is much easier to find out if an animal can *respond* differently to red and green than it is to answer the question of what it 'feels like' to the animal to see red or green colours.

Having shown that it was helpful to ignore the subjective impressions of animals, Watson strongly recommended this strategy to psychologists in general. The methodology of measuring what people do, instead of trying to measure what people say they feel, became very widely used even by psychologists who did not agree with other theories that Watson put forward. This practice of relying on behavioural evidence is the crucial aspect of *behaviourism*, which was the name given by Watson to his recommendations.

The importance of learning. One of Watson's theories was that all human skills, personality traits and motives are learned. He argued against the view that abilities 'run in families' because they are inherited, and against the idea that there are inherited psychological differences between races. Nothing of any psychological importance is inherited in Watson's opinion, but all psychological differences between individuals are due to differences in upbringing, training or past experience. After showing that Pavlovian conditioning procedures could change the emotional preferences of babies (see Ch. 3). Watson came to the conclusion that even complex aspects of adult personality were the products of 'millions of conditionings'.

It is still characteristic of behaviourists to believe that processes of learning pervade human life. Learning in this sense is not just something that happens when you set about 'learning French' or 'learning to play tennis'. It is something which happens continually, whether you like it or not, and modifies your behaviour towards other people and changes your opinions as well as operating in a more obvious manner to improve skills or academic ability. Watson's version of Sechenov's slogan would be 'all acts of conscious or unconscious life are determined by learning'.

Thorndike and the Law of Effect

Thorndike was a contemporary of Watson's whose work was often quoted in Watson's books. However, Thorndike had his own independent theories about learning, and the most influential of these was expressed in his *Law of Effect* which was based on his early experiments with animals. Thorndike was attracted to psychology by reading William James' *Principles*, and went as a postgraduate student to Harvard, where James was preparing to change back to professor of philosophy from professor of psychology. Despite his shift back to philosophy, it was James who, when Thorndike was turned out of his lodgings for hatching chickens in the bedroom, gave the young Thorndike and the chickens room in his own home. Thorndike's experiments on learning in chicks were repeated with cats and dogs, and produced the Law of Effect, which applies to voluntary movements and behaviour. In the experiments animals were left inside a 'puzzle-box' to solve the problem of how to get out. The solution involved finding and operating a latch. The results persuaded Thorndike (1898) that, although the animals eventually became adept at escaping from confinement, they did not do it by some form of reasoning or thought but by automatically remembering accidental successes. Cats, for instance, might cry and scratch and turn around in the box in an unsystematic way, eventually being let out when they scratched at the latch. But this does not produce a realization by the cat that 'to get out one has to scratch the latch'. On being put back in the box the cat again scratches and turns at random. Learning does take place, but only by gradual adjustments to behaviour so that over a sequence of twenty attempts the cat escapes slightly more quickly each time.

According to the Law of Effect, the improvement comes about because the actions which work the latch are gradually strengthened by the success, pleasure or satisfaction produced by getting out of the box (which is the 'effect' of the actions).

The systematic behaviour theory of C. L. Hull

Hull tried to bring together the findings of Pavlov and Thorndike and use them as the basis of a very special kind of theory. He was an experienced psychologist by the time he started this, having published books on aptitude testing and hypnosis. But he became fascinated by the idea of constructing psychological laws that were not vague suggestions but mathematical equations. Pavlov and Thorndike had demonstrated that scientific methods of measurement could be applied to learned behaviour, and Hull advocated that these measurements could be used to sustain a type of theory more like theories in physics. In his last attempt to construct a system like this himself (Hull, 1952) there were thirty-two equations, but the main one of general application was this:

$$_sE_R = D \times V \times K \times {_sH_R}$$

It means that the intensity or likelihood of any item of learned behaviour ($_sE_R$) can be calculated if four other factors are known: the drive or motivation associated with it (D), the intensity of the signal for the behaviour (V), the degree of incentive used (K) and the degree of habit ($_sH_R$). Under controlled laboratory conditions all the factors can be measured, and the equation checked: $_sE_R$ by the probability or intensity of response, drive by hours of deprivation or physical need, incentive by the level of reward used, and habit by the amount of practice given.

The ideals behind the theory, and the possibility of confirming or disproving theories by laboratory experiment, made Hull's theory extremely influential for a number of years. However, most of the equations were found to be of limited application, if not incorrect, and enthusiasm for such an ambitious approach has waned. Nonetheless, many of the innovations and suggestions made by Hull have survived and his goal of a 'hypothetico-deductive' theory of psychology, which allows precise predictions to be made and tested, has not been totally abandoned, especially for use on a small scale.

E. C. Tolman – behaviourism with thinking

Tolman was a behaviourist in so far as he accepted only precise measurements of behaviour as evidence, but he would nowadays be called a 'cognitive' theorist, since he inferred from his evidence that his animal subjects had thoughts, in the form of 'expectancies', 'insights', 'cognitive maps' and 'hypotheses'. He narrowed the gap between animals and men by attributing thought processes to animals, like Darwin, rather than emphasizing automatic processes in man like Sechenov. Behaviourists are often accused of mistaking their evidence for the substance of their inquiries, and Tolman's work was an important corrective against this tendency. There is a difference between knowing and doing even for laboratory rats, as Tolman demonstrated in a variety of experiments which measured rats' proficiency at finding their way around ingeniously-designed mazes.

Latent learning. Tolman and Honzik (1930) demonstrated that rats could find their way about in a maze during idle exploration, so that when they were motivated to get out of the maze quickly, by use of a food reward at the end, little additional learning was necessary. After this the distinction between the experiences necessary for *learning*, and the conditions which favour the *performance* of learned behaviour, received more emphasis. It is incorporated for instance into Hull's equation given above, in that the reward factor and the practice factor are kept separate.

Cognitive maps. Tolman suggested that an important part of learning is knowledge of 'what-leads-to-what', which he termed an *expectancy*. This is an alternative to Hull's concept of habit, and emphasizes that information about the environment can be acquired independently of particular responses to the environment. The maze-solving abilities of rats imply that rats learn something *about* the maze; having learned to run around a maze, they may for instance be able to swim successfully around a similar maze, or negotiate the maze backwards. Tolman said that this ability was due to the formation of 'cognitive maps' by the animals, which could be used later to guide various kinds of movements.

16

Skinner's radical behaviourism

Although Skinner's first book appeared in 1938, his work is currently the most influential of any psychologist in the field of learning. This is partly because he himself is continuing to supply important theoretical contributions and provocative statements of his views on the implication of his findings for the public at large (Skinner, 1971, 1974). There is also much work being done by others directly in the Skinnerian tradition, both in the sense of laboratory experiment and in other applications. However, it is also arguable that Skinner's influence is necessarily less subject to shifts of opinion or advances in other fields, in so far as it depends largely on experimental fact rather than speculative explanations. Although he himself does not do so, it is worth separating Skinner's innovations in laboratory methods and procedures, and his discoveries of experimental facts, from his philosophical position on the use and implication of these methods and facts.

Facts of operant conditioning. By repeatedly giving small bits of food to hungry animals, Skinner demonstrated the practical effects of these food rewards extremely dramatically. He calls these effects *positive reinforcement*, and the bits of food *reinforcers*. The drama was supplied by careful training of individual animals in complex tasks. This can be done simply by positive reinforcement, if a little-by-little method is used to develop gradually or *shape* the behaviour of the subject towards the final form. For instance, Skinner trained a rat to release a marble by pulling a string, and then to carry the marble away and drop it in a tin. This is a fairly difficult task for a rat, and the rat cannot easily be told or shown what to do. But the information can be conveyed, in the limited sense that the rat learns what to do, by the use of the shaping procedure (sometimes termed *successive approximation*). For instance, the rat might never lift the marble to drop it in the can without training, but Skinner started with a can only a fraction of an inch high, and when the rat had learned, by being reinforced, to lift the marble that distance, increased the height. After several small increases, the rat had learned to make the complete lift.

In addition to such demonstrations, Skinner developed more general experimental methods. In contrast to Thorndike, who conducted experiments in his bedroom (which housed several species of animal as well as Thorndike), Skinner, like Pavlov, used carefully-controlled laboratory conditions. Animals were typically isolated from outside disturbance by being placed inside a special sound-proofed chamber (often called a 'Skinner box'). The standard procedure was to use the delivery of pellets of food to make a rat press the lever in the box, with automatic devices to record presses of the lever and to deliver the reinforcer. By isolating these two variables, the response of pressing the lever and the reinforcer of food delivery, it was possible to observe how completely the reinforcer controlled the response (see Ch. 4). *Contingencies of reinforcement* are fixed relations between the response, the reinforcer and signals presented to the subject. One kind of contingency is the *schedule of reinforcement*, a straight-forward rule about the delivery of reinforcers such as 'a reinforcer is delivered at every third response'. Skinner's discovery is that contingencies of reinforcement exert an extremely powerful influence on behaviour.

Skinner's extrapolations. Having established the intimate relationship between behaviour and contingencies of reinforcement in the laboratory, Skinner has gone on to assert the importance of these contingencies in every aspect of psychology. It is fair to paraphrase Skinner's views in the Sechenov form: 'All acts of conscious or unconscious life are determined by contingencies of reinforcement'.

Skinner now makes a further leap of imagination. He insists that in government, education and economics, matters can be much improved if contingencies of reinforcement are designed so as to produce desired behaviours. He suggests that Utopia is indeed attainable by the use of such methods (Skinner, 1971). There may be something in this, and extreme positions are often necessary to make a point. But it is possible to distinguish very sharply between what has been established in the laboratory, what looks promising in some applied fields, and what are Skinner's visions and extrapolations.

The evidence to show that contingencies of reinforcement control behaviour under laboratory conditions is overwhelming. It seems quite probable that principles derived from laboratory conditions can be helpful in some aspects of education and mental health. However, there is absolutely no evidence to show that principles discovered by Skinner are appropriate for large-scale application in politics and economics. It is therefore not surprising that there are reservations about using Skinner's 'test-tube' methods in these complicated and sensitive areas of real life.

Radical behaviourism. Another extreme position taken by Skinner may stand him in better stead. This is his self-restraint in the matter of speculative explanations. Explanations of why or how contingencies of reinforcement work would be interesting, but Skinner has avoided making any. His point is that descriptions of behaviour, and relations between behaviour and variables we can be certain of, are reliable, and are sufficient explanations in themselves.

We may want to know how our behaviour is related to (a) our subjective experience and (b) the activity of our brains. Skinner suggests that (a) our subjective experience is simply a kind of behaviour and (b) knowledge of physiology will not change the behavioural facts. This radical position has worked to Skinner's advantage in that the behavioural facts which he emphasized have not become outdated because of advances in neurophysiology or changes in theories of cognition. However, it is likely that as knowledge about the physiology of the brain increases, the advantages of ignoring it will diminish.

Conclusions and summary

Since Darwin and Sechenov, scientists have been giving radical answers to various riddles about human existence. Darwin's claim that the human species had evolved from other animal species is now generally accepted, and there are many psychologists who agree with his argument that evolution applies just as well to psychology as to anatomy. Behaviourists especially, since they discount subjective impressions, usually stress the continuity between human and animal behaviour. The riddle of man's obviously more varied behaviour has been given the answer of 'learning', man being supposed to learn faster and better, though not differently, from other animals. Consequently, a good deal of attention has been devoted to the study of learning in animals, because of this background assumption that learning is important for the rest of psychology.

The remaining chapters are about the different sorts of learning which have been studied experimentally, with examples of how facts discovered in this way are currently being applied to alleviate problems in human behaviour.

2
Habituation: the difference between familiar and unfamiliar stimuli

Reading this book and understanding it should be an example of quite an advanced form of learning. But if reading it merely helps you to fall asleep, that is an example of a much more elementary form of learning, *habituation*. As a simple form of learning habituation is being studied now, in primitive animals rather than readers of books, by scientists interested in the essential physiological changes that enable learning to occur (see A2). The usual form of habituation is the repeated exposure to the same stimulus that makes for very sluggish responses to that stimulus, but in some cases the lack of responsiveness does indeed blend into a state of sleep. In this chapter habituation will serve as an example in several issues which apply more widely: the use of the terms *stimulus* and *response*; the difference between behavioural processes and physiological processes; and the co-existence of elementary with more elaborate forms of learning.

Stimulus (S) and response (R)

Stimulus and response are descriptive units for behaviour, often abbreviated to S and R. If someone sticks a pin in you and this makes you jump, the pin-prick may be termed the 'stimulus' and your jump the 'response'. The fact that people normally jump when stuck with pins might be referred to as a 'stimulus-response relationship'. Even in this simple example there are many questions that can be asked about what is really going on: What exactly is the stimulus? Is it the pin, the insertion of the pin, the activation of nerve-endings in the skin, or the subjective feeling of the pin-prick? Is the response the twitching of particular muscles or any sudden body movement? Different answers are possible, and the terms 'stimulus' and 'response' are used in a variety of specialized ways. But the most common use is merely as a convenient distinction between things an organism may be confronted with and activities which it might display. Most psychologists would accept this distinction in the case of pins and jumping: 'people normally jump when stuck with a pin' would be accepted as a stimulus-response relationship. The bone of contention comes in when more complicated cases are seen in stimulus-response terms. 'If you talk to someone, they will usually talk back' is true enough, but 'the stimulus of talking to someone will usually lead to the response of their talking back' still raises some hackles. However, with most cases of habituation, and other simple forms of learning, it is practically impossible to give an account of what happens without distinguishing between things which are there in the environment (stimuli) and things which the subject does (responses).

Concentrating on stimulus-response relationships is typical of behaviourists, and is useful in the study of learning when learning is judged to be a *change* in behaviour. The kinds of learning which are easiest to measure are those identified by a change in a single stimulus-response (S-R) relation. In habituation the change is that an animal or person *ceases* to react to a stimulus, and in classical conditioning (Ch. 3) the subject *begins* to react to a stimulus. Because very systematic measurements can be made of these elementary changes in stimulus-response relations, such S-R relationships are often taken as basic units of learning, as if they were atoms or molecules which can be assembled into more elaborate skills. In some cases theorists such as Hull (see p. 15) have assumed that all kinds of behaviour, however complex, are composed of S-R units. The difficulty in this is that in order to encompass any reasonably intelligent behaviour, it has to be assumed that there are hypothetical S-R units at work inside the head, which cannot themselves be measured. That spoils the original advantage of the S-R description, which was that it was based on accurate observations. In any case, it has turned out that S-R theories do not apply very well to complicated activities like problem-solving (see A7). But, although S-R *theories* have limited application, this does not mean that it is necessary to abandon S-R *descriptions*. The topic of habituation demonstrates this point rather well: habituation cries out to be described as the decline in responsiveness to a stimulus, but one of the main *theories* of habituation says that this ultra-simple behavioural change comes about because of exceedingly complicated goings-on inside the head, which have little to do with S-R units (see p. 25). We can continue to talk of stimulus-response relations without committing ourselves to any particular explanations as to what physiological mechanisms are doing the job of governing the vigour of responses to a particular stimulus input.

Changes in response when a stimulus is presented repeatedly: habituation and 'warm-up' effects

The most rudimentary case of changed response to a repeated stimulus occurs with single nerve fibres (see A2). A nerve fibre can be made to respond, producing an impulse which travels down the fibre, by a standard electrical stimulus. But immediately after this, it remains completely unresponsive (the absolute refractory period) and then goes through a phase of being less responsive than usual (the relative refactory period). Obviously this is far removed from learning and is more a matter of taking time to recover the physical ability to make a response. Decline in response due to muscular fatigue has some similar characteristics; if you jumped when someone said jump, the vigour of your jumping would wane if the stimulus were frequently repeated, if for no other reason than muscular tiredness.

A second kind of drop in response with repeated stimulation is *sensory adaption*. The best example of sensory adaption is the reaction of the eye to strong lights: the pupil contracts to let less light into the eye and the retina of the eye becomes less sensitive. The effect takes some time to wear off so that, if you move a light into a much darker environment, things get gradually clearer and clearer: if for instance you go into a cinema on a sunny afternoon it is much harder to see the way to the seat at first than it would be ten minutes later.

The decline in response called *habituation* occurs over and above any response decrements due to sensory adaptation or muscular fatigue and is much more interesting psychologically than these two effects. In most cases habituation can be conceived as a lessening of response produced by the increasing familiarity of a stimulus. If a friend stops putting up counter-arguments when you state your pet political theory, this does not mean necessarily that he has been temporarily deafened or that he is too tired to talk, it may be because he has heard it all before, and it has become so familiar that it fails to stir him. You might say that he had become habituated to your theory (even if he still disagrees with it).

There is in fact a wealth of examples from a wide range of human and animal behaviour where isolated responses wane as the stimulus which provokes them recurs, without the intervention of muscular fatigue or sensory adaption (Hinde, 1970). However, the scope of habituation is so comprehensive, embracing almost every type of behaviour, that as Hinde says the 'underlying processes' must vary enormously.

At one extreme, investigations of the sea-slug *Aplysia* have revealed that the habituation of its gill-withdrawal reflex depends to a large extent on the changes at synapses between sensory and motor nerve cells. A jet of sea-water squirted at a sensitive area near the gills would normally make the gills withdraw, but this reflex habituates after five to ten squirts given within a few minutes of each other. The independence of this habituation from adaptation or fatigue can be demonstrated because a strong squirt of sea-water to another part of the body brings back the full gill-withdrawal response to local stimulation (this is called *dishabituation*). Essentially the same habituation and dishabituation could be observed in decapitated slugs or, by taking electrical recordings from sensory and motor neurons, in a surgically isolated *Aplysia* abdominal ganglion (Castellucci *et al.*, 1970). This work tells us something about the minimal nervous system equipment which can accomplish the behavioural changes involved in habituation. The same kind of behavioural changes, in terms of increases and decreases in responsiveness to stimuli, can also be brought about in animals with much more complicated nervous systems and indeed with ordinary human subjects, as the next section shows. This is a very striking example of how similar stimulus-response relationships can arise from different underlying processes. It may be perfectly true to say that 'the response declines when the stimulus is repeated' or 'the response habituates' in a wide variety of situations, even if the reasons behind the habituation are not always the same.

Surprise, alertness and the orienting reflex

Despite the variety of responses which are covered by the behavioural definition of habituation, it is possible to isolate some general features of habituation in what Pavlov called the 'what is it?' reflex, which has been studied in man and other mammals. Any very unfamiliar or unexpected stimulus will produce the 'orienting reflex'. A fairly intense stimulus such as an explosion or thunderclap may make one literally jump or lead to flinching of the whole body. Less extreme stimuli may nevertheless produce easily visible responses such as turning or looking towards the source of the stimulus. Animals may 'prick up their ears' especially to strange sounds, and people 'look surprised' when something unexpected happens.

Physiological expressions of surprise. The immediately visible reactions to strange stimuli are not the only ones available for the psychologist to measure. Indices of autonomic nervous system activity such as pulse rate and skin resistance, as well as general muscle tension and electrical brainwaves (see A2) all show changes when a new stimulus occurs. A good deal of research has been done, especially by scientists influenced by Pavlovian traditions, such as Sokolov (1963), on the way in which these physiological manifestations of the orienting reflex change as stimuli are presented over and over again to a human subject. Sokolov uses three categories of response: first, *adaptation reflexes*, mainly specialized reflexes allowing for adjustments of sensory systems (such as the contraction of the pupil of the eye for high levels of illumination); second, the *defensive reflexes* to high intensity or painful stimulation; and finally, for lower stimulus intensities, the *orienting reflex*, distinguished by the fact that it occurs in response to new stimuli, and declines as a given stimulus is repeated to the same person. Components of the orienting reflex include an increase in sensory sensitivity, a drop in skin resistance, increased indications of arousal in the EEG (the electroencephalogram of brainwaves), constriction of blood vessels in the limbs, dilation of blood vessels in the head and a lowering of respiration and pulse rates.

The 'neuronal model' of stimuli. The main point about the

orienting reflex is that it shows a progressive reduction as a stimulus gains in familiarity through repetition. But slight changes in the stimulus when the orienting reflex has completely disappeared will be sufficient to bring it back. That is, a familiar stimulus can become surprising again if there is a quite small change in it.

Sokolov has put forward a theory to explain this which assumes that a 'neuronal model' or physical memory of each stimulus is built up by repeated experience. The orienting reflex is produced when a stimulus is given for which there is no model, but declines as the model for that stimulus is built up. Habituation results when there is a complete match between the stimulus received and the internal model. This theory explains why quite small changes in a familiar stimulus could lead to 'surprise' in Sokolov's experiments. It also helps to explain the 'missing stimulus effect' Sokolov found. To show this effect, a subject is presented with the same stimulus at regular intervals until there is no flicker of response to be measured. Then the stimulus is missed out, and the subject shows the surprise reaction at the time when it was due. It seems as though there is some form of temporal conditioning (see Ch. 3) which can take place even during habituation, and which becomes part of the 'neuronal model'. Thus when a stimulus presentation is missed out, there is a 'mismatch' and the subject notices the absence. This is rather like being kept awake by the ticking of a clock, eventually falling asleep, only to be woken up when the clock stops.

'Warm-up' or sensitization effects

Although the neuronal model theory deals with the fact that familiar stimuli are ignored, while unfamiliar happenings rouse orienting reactions, it does not explain very well those cases where there are *sensitization* effects, which are opposite to the effects of habituation. Some experiments which help to clarify the distinction between habituation and sensitization have been conducted on the 'startle response' evoked in rats by loud noise. In experiments of this kind, the rat is tested in a small soundproofed cage equipped with electronic devices which can pick up any sudden movements it makes. Habituation to loud tones can then be expressed in terms of changes in the number and vigour of the startle responses. Anyone who has lived for a time near a large airport knows that hearing a noise in the 100 to 120 dB range can be both startling and disturbing. They are two opposite ways in which exposure to repeated loud noise can change this startle response. There is some degree of habituation or 'getting used to it' over time, so that long-term residents near airports may be less disturbed by passing jets than their guests from a quieter area. But there is also a cumulative effect, so that at the end of a particularly noisy weekend, even hardened residents may be more 'jumpy' than at the beginning. By using sounds in the 'jet taking off' range, these two effects of cumulative exposure have been clearly identified in rats who were exposed to loud tones in eight thirty-minute sessions spaced out over four weeks (Davis, 1972).

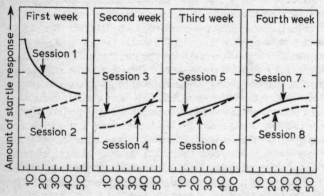

Fig. 2.1 *Habituation and sensitization of startle.* Amount of startle during eight sessions. Fifty very loud blips were given each session, thirty seconds apart. (After Davis, 1972)

As can be seen in Figure 2.1 the rats 'got used' to the noise in that they were less startled in successive sessions. But there was also a temporary sensitizing effect within each half-hour session, so that after the first one the rats were more startled at the end than at the beginning of a session.

Habituation by degrees. The sensitization process may be responsible for another curious effect found with startle responses. This is that gradual increases in noise level serve as an exceptionally effective way of producing habituation to loud noises. If rats are exposed first to a moderately loud noise, and then to a sequence of gradually increasing loudness, they show much less response to a very loud noise than animals given an equivalent period of training with either the very loud noise itself, or just a moderate sound, or a random series of noises. This kind of effect means that other factors, apart from the 'neuronal model' or stimulus memory aspect of habituation, help to determine the level of response. The best guess at present seems to be that the 'gradual increase' procedure allows the rats to keep in a relatively calm *state* of some kind or other, while habituation is taking place. In other words, a tolerance of noises in general can be built up without increased excitability or sensitivity entering in as much as usual. It is easy to think of the 'calm state' as being lack of annoyance or anxiety, but this is another case where 'state of excitability' may take several physiological forms.

Arousal, interest and sleep

That general states of arousal are closely connected with the orienting reflex and habituation was emphasized by Pavlov, who found that repetition of sounds of little interest to the dogs used in his experiments made the dogs go to sleep. Habituation to particular stimuli seems to reduce arousal, if no alternative interesting stimuli are available. Repetitious stimulation, obtained by counting imaginary sheep or reading dull books, is widely accepted as an aid to sleep, and similar effects have been found in laboratory experiments. But counting sheep will not be relaxing for a worried sheep farmer, because for him sheep are an important stimulus, having an arousing rather than sleep-inducing effect. For particular people and species of animal there are different stimulus categories, some stimuli being danger signals, or aversive; others being positively interesting or rewarding; and others being relatively unimportant, provided that they are familiar. Habituation to the extent of decreasing arousal applies mainly to relatively neutral situations, that is stimuli which have little significance in the basic motivational systems. Thus for animals stimuli associated with food, sex or pain are less likely to habituate than random noises in the laboratory, and lectures or books that are boring for one person may be intensely interesting to another.

It has been suggested that curiosity, which represents the absence of habituation, is itself motivating. Although the first reaction of animals to strange stimuli is usually fear and withdrawal, the next reaction is some degree of curiosity, exploration, and after sufficient investigation, 'curiosity is satisfied', i.e. there is habituation. According to Berlyne (1969) level of arousal (in terms of alertness as opposed to drowsiness) acts as a motivating system because there is an *optimal* level of arousal. In a state of high arousal, familiar situations, or stimuli which have habituated, will be actively preferred, because they will bring arousal back to a more tolerable level, but in a state of low arousal novel and even dangerous stimuli will be sought out precisely because they raise the arousal level – or supply relief from boredom. As an extreme case, people will seek out dangerous activities such as parachuting or mountain-climbing for 'excitement' as well as finding excitement more safely by watching films of disaster or horror. But for relatively neutral stimuli, the process of fashion in clothes and music provide examples of how important 'novelty' can be in a stimulus. There are undoubtedly a great many complicating factors, but possibly habituation is one of the reasons why popular records decline in popularity when they have been heard over and over again. It is also often suggested that fads and fashions influence the popularity of psychological theories, so that even a fairly sound theory may be replaced by a new one because psychologists prefer novelty!

Habituation and satiation. Powerful motivating stimuli tend not to habituate, but this is probably more a case of the motivating effects masking any habituation which does take place. If you are starving, then your experience of food stimuli will not produce any noticeable reduction in your interest in food. However, most people at what we regard as normal levels of hunger would quickly habituate to particular foods. You may like pork-pies, but if you were to eat nothing else for a couple of weeks you would surely like them a good deal less. This is *stimulus satiation* for pork-pies. But it is worth distinguishing this stimulus factor from 'after eating' satiation, which would occur if you at half a dozen pork-pies at once. Specialized physiological processes ensure that you would be 'satiated', presumably for all foods, for a few hours after that. Food satiation is basically a short term physical influence, like muscular fatigue. Nevertheless, if you make yourself sick by eating chocolates you should be 'put-off' chocolates for some time afterwards.

With important social and sexual stimuli, habituation and satiation may be entangled with other factors. 'Absence makes the heart grow fonder' may refer to a state of social deprivation, or to cases where affectional responses recover from habituation as the object of the affections becomes less familiar. Eysenck (1973) has suggested that the search for social and sexual novelty is an aspect of the 'extrovert' personality, which having a low level of arousal requires the maximum of excitement from external sources. An opposite kind of influence, which Eysenck would say is more prevalent for introverted persons, is the desire to be reassured constantly by well-known social contacts and familiar surroundings.

One may conclude that habituation, sensitization and satiation, resulting simply from how often certain stimuli have been experienced, either in the recent past or over a long period, may be at the bottom of many emotional preferences, drives or reinforcers. Curiosity and a craving for novelty, or a need for the security of accustomed environments and habits are at opposite ends of a motivational system based on habituation, but long-past or recent experience of stimuli may modify a great many other motives.

Habituation in therapy

There are a number of techniques used in behaviour therapy (see F3) which involve an element of habituation. In the negative practice method (see below) repetition of response is the critical variable, in other methods the frequent or prolonged presentation of a stimulus may be a factor, and in the desensitization procedure (p. 30) the 'gradual increase' sequence appears. These kinds of therapy are relevant here because they all make use of the repetition of stimuli and responses and an ingredient such as boredom, satiation or increased stimulus familiarity.

Negative practice. It has often been claimed that annoying habits such as tics could be treated by intensive repetition (Meyer and Chesser, 1970). A patient who wishes to be rid of a nervous tic may be told to produce it deliberately as accurately and frequently as possible for a period of several minutes. There are several reports of successful reduction of tic frequency after this simple expedient of deliberate repetition. Another problem which has been helped by this treatment is a rare neurological condition involving pathological use of obscene words. In this case the patient was required to repeat an obscenity over and over again, in time to a metronome.

Stimulus satiation. Allyon (1963) treated a patient who had been in hospital for nine years and usually managed to keep twenty or thirty towels in her room despite the efforts of nursing staff to recover them. The treatment was for the staff to give the patient as many towels as she would accept, instead of removing them. She accepted 625 before beginning to refuse additional towels. It took four weeks to accumulate this number but during the next ten weeks the patient gradually discarded towels, until she finally kept only one or two. This more ordinary requirement was maintained during the subsequent year of observation. At the same time this patient was taught to refrain from her previous habits of stealing other patients' food and wearing several sets of clothes. The overall effect was to allow more normal social interaction between the patient and other people in the hospital.

Desensitization. This method of therapy has been in widespread use for about twenty years. The symptom most frequently treated by desensitization is a phobia or excessive fear of such things as spiders, traffic or heights. One of the main features of the therapy is that the therapist helps the patient to form a 'hierarchy' or gradual progression of problem situations starting with stimuli that are just tolerable and progressing to situations which would cause panic or extreme anxiety and stress for the patient. When desensitization was first used, relaxation training was often a preliminary stage of therapy and the main stage consisted of the patient relaxing at the same time as *imagining* the problem situation, starting with the less severe forms at the bottom of the hierarchy, and working upwards until even the worst scene could be imagined without disturbance. In this case, using imagined problem situations, it was found that the relaxation training is an important part of the procedure (Paul, 1969) and it seems as though the conditioning of relaxation is the basis for success (see Ch. 3).

Real-life (or *in vivo*) situations have been used instead of imagined scenes, and here relaxation training is not as important as 'getting used to' feared stimuli (habituation), which plays a large part. For instance, a patient may be severely distressed by fear of large hairy spiders, to the extent of not being able to go anywhere remotely likely to be harbouring a spider. Desensitization has been achieved in such cases by means of a collection of real spiders of various sizes. The patient first 'gets used to' being at close quarters with a small hairless spider and then is confronted with a succession of increasingly hairy and monstrous ones. When techniques like this succeed it appears that graded exposure to real problem situations can be sufficient in itself to abolish extreme emotional reactions.

Flooding. There are some neurotic complaints where the 'little-by-little' desensitization method does not work, perhaps because the source of anxiety cannot be equated with a hierarchy of external stimuli like small to large spiders. Agoraphobia, fear of being in the open or fear of going out, is one problem where desensitization has been tried without much success, but it responds to an alternative procedure called *flooding*. In flooding a stimulus hierarchy is not critical, because the basis of the method is to maintain an extremely high level of anxiety until some process of exhaustion or stimulus satiation intervenes. It is obviously necessary to be very careful about using a procedure causing distress during treatment, but a number of investigations have indicated that flooding may be worthwhile both in agoraphobia and in obsessive-compulsive disorders.

Emmelkamp and Wessels (1975) suggested that agoraphobia may be relieved by flooding, especially if an *in vivo* method is used. This amounted to long walks taken by the patient, starting off from his home and taking a difficult route going directly away from home, as agreed previously with the therapist, without being allowed to take a dog or familiar item such as an umbrella to relieve the tension. For comparison, imaginal flooding consisted of sessions lasting as long as the walks (ninety minutes) in which the patient was asked to visualize as vividly as possible fear-provoking scenes described by the therapist. A behavioural test of the effect of these therapies was made by asking patients to stay outside for as long as they felt comfortable. Patients who panicked after a few minutes before treatment were able to stay outside for about an hour after the forced exposure of long walks, but those given the treatment by imagination showed relatively little improvement.

When flooding is used in therapy for chronic obsessive compulsive neurosis, it is very important that the patient be prevented from engaging in his usual compulsive rituals in situations designed deliberately to provoke the rituals (Hodgson et al., 1972). A common obsession is the fear of contamination, which is connected with rituals to avoid contact with the feared source of contamination (animals, for instance) and compulsive hand-washing and cleaning. In the use of flooding for this obsession a patient might be encouraged to forbear avoidance or cleaning activities while staying in a room with several cats and dogs and having hamsters crawl over their clothes and hair. Exposure to the extreme case may enable the patient to cope with everyday situations, provided that the extreme case is tolerated without the usual compulsive actions. It seems that good results are also obtained, at less cost to the patient, if it is the *therapist* who must have hamsters in his hair, while the patient watches, at least for part of the treatment. This vicarious exposure to the problem situation (see Ch. 9) may help by making it easier for the patient to withhold his compulsive responses while becoming accustomed to previously disturbing events. But in one way or another, it looks as though flooding bears some similarity to a procedure for habituation; for it is a repeated exposure to a particular situation which leads to a decline in behaviours which were initially an inevitable product of the stimulus.

Summary and conclusions

The idle repetition of a stimulus in the environment which initially provokes some activity or alertness changes sensitivity to the stimulus. The main result is a shut-down of sensitivity to the stimulus, called habituation, but there may also be short-term increases in sensitivity, called sensitization. Habituation is a form of learning in so far as the current response, or lack of response, depends on previous experiences. When it is a matter of becoming familiar with stimuli, and being interested in the new as opposed to the old, habituation may reflect the learning of many complex features of familiar items. It is often useful to be able to ignore stimuli, especially as an alternative to being made over-anxious by them, and therefore some of the behavioural procedures for reducing anxiety – such as desensitization and flooding – mirror the habituation process.

3
Classical conditioning: involuntary associations

The method of classical conditioning is based on Pavlov's work, which was briefly introduced in Chapter 1. Pavlov himself was usually fairly cautious in his claims, but did make one or two comments to the effect that many forms of action were 'nothing but' collections of conditioned reflexes. There is still considerable debate about how far the results obtained by Pavlov apply to everyday life. Some of the issues in this debate are sketched in here, before we look at Pavlov's findings.

Operant conditioning and classical conditioning. One rather theoretical problem is whether or not one may classify different types of conditioning. There is some measure of agreement on the possibility of distinguishing two different laboratory techniques: *operant* and *classical* conditioning. Operant conditioning is described in detail in the next two chapters, and some of the distinctions between it and Pavlov's methods will be obvious. The main factor is whether or not striving to achieve a goal is a characteristic of the behaviour which has been conditioned. Although this is a very loose way of talking about conditioning, it is a good rule of thumb for choosing between the technicalities of the two types. If the conditioned behaviour is essentially a rather inflexible and automatic reaction to a particular stimulus or situation, then it is more likely to relate to *classical* conditioning. But if there is some achieving of goals, avoidance of punishment, or even unrewarded striving, we are more likely to talk about *operant* or *instrumental* conditioning (see Chs. 3 and 4).

Responses that can be classically conditioned. Pavlov's first experiments were with the response of salivary secretion, and by and large classical (or 'Pavlovian') conditioning applies best to involuntary or emotional reactions. Many of these have the distinction of being controlled by a special part of the nervous system, the 'autonomic nervous system' (see A2), which usually deals with digestion, breathing and so on and does not involve much conscious effort. Many responses that we can almost never be directly aware of may easily be conditioned: changes in electrical resistance of the skin, changes in heart rate, blood pressure and various types of electrical brain rhythms. Many of these 'autonomic' responses, such as skin resistance and heart rate, are closely connected with emotional states, and it seems inevitable that at least some of our more 'reflexive' emotional reactions are coloured by classically-conditioned associations. Visual symbols such as national flags, the swastika, hammer and sickle, or cross usually have a very direct emotional impact, apart from any reasoned considerations that may be added on to it. Words with powerful associations may also elicit direct emotional reactions before we have had time to 'think about the words: e.g. fascist; IRA, sex, unemployment. Generally speaking, emotional reactions and individually classically-conditioned responses are involuntary, in that it is very difficult to decide to salivate, or be angry, or in the absence of any appropriate stimulus; it is also very difficult to decide *not* to salivate or be angry if a strong signal for those reactions occurs. With sufficient training and practice, actors may decide to have any of a range of emotional reactions, and physiological tests have confirmed that expert yogis in India can make voluntary decisions about autonomic responses such as blood pressure and heart rate. But there is a monumental difference in degree between the difficulty of such expert control and the unavoidable simplicity of conditioned emotional associations.

Experiments in classical conditioning

The clearest example of an experiment which shows classical conditioning uncontaminated with other factors is the one showing that involuntary knee jerks could be conditioned to the sound of a bell, if the bell was always rung before the knee was tapped. The unconditioned stimulus (US or UCS) of the tap on the knee has relatively few effects on the subject apart from the one intended. However, giving food to hungry dogs, as Pavlov did, may have many other psyhcological effects apart from eliciting salivation. The dog may enjoy the experiment far more than one where painful stimuli were used, and wag its tail and strain towards the food bowl when the conditioned stimulus is presented. A popular method of studying classical conditioning in human subjects is that of linking eyeblink responses to sounds or faint lights by making these stimuli signals for a short puff of air to the eye. People who undergo this procedure start by blinking when air is puffed at their eye, but soon begin to blink when a signal which precedes the air puffs is presented. A problem with this method is that blinking occurs every few seconds as a matter of course, and blinking may also be done voluntarily, or nervously, by some subjects.

Notwithstanding these difficulties, a wide range of techniques have been developed with laboratory animals such as

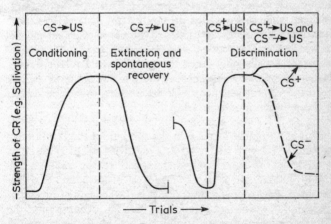

Fig. 3.1 *Various phases of classical conditioning.* The progress of conditioning is marked by changes in the strength of the CR (conditioned response) e.g. the number of drops of saliva secreted when a stimulus is presented. In conditioning the CS is always followed by the UCS and then in extinction the CS is given by itself. In discrimination one stimulus is a signal for the UCS but a second stimulus is not.

rats, pigeons and monkeys, and data collected by these methods, together with the data from human subjects, provide a wealth of evidence by which to judge Pavlov's original discoveries. Although new aspects of conditioning have been investigated, and many new theories to explain classical conditioning have been put forward, the great mass of accumulated data confirms facts of conditioning named by Pavlov and his contemporaries.

The Pavlovian experiment

In the conditioning apparatus used by Pavlov a dog is loosely restrained on a stand with a tube running from its cheek to allow very precise measurement of the volume of saliva it secretes. It is hungry, and every five minutes or so a small door opens in front of it and a small amount of food is pushed out. When the dog sees the food it starts to salivate, and this can be measured by the experimenter from recording apparatus in the next room. The experimenter has remote control of buzzer and lights and similar signalling devices, so that a signal can regularly be presented just before the food, or at other times.

Acquisition of the conditioned response. This term is commonly used for what Pavlov called the establishing or development of the conditioned reflex. It applies to the phase of an experiment in which the CS (conditioned stimulus) begins to provoke responses usually only given to the UCS. In Pavlov's experiments this would be the phase where a dog starts to salivate when the CS, for instance an electric buzzer, sounds, as well as salivating when food is presented.

Figure 3.1 shows how the initial acquisition phase can be plotted as a gradual increase in the strength of the conditioned response (CR) from trial to trial. (*Trial* is often used in the sense of trial run, to refer to a presentation of the experimental stimuli.) Although it is the changes in response that are measured, Pavlov emphasized that it is the changing function of the stimulus which is theoretically vital. The acquisition of the CR can be interpreted as 'stimulus-substitution', since the CS comes to serve as a substitute for the UCS. We might put it rather loosely this way: in a Pavlovian experiment the dog learns that the CS means food.

Extinction and spontaneous recovery. Suppose that after acquisi-

36

tion, when the CS was accompanied by food, the CS were to be presented over and over again without any food. Would the dog go on salivating? In some circumstances (see Chs. 4 and 5) a CR may persist for a remarkably long time. However, as a rule in the Pavlovian experiment, the CR diminishes quickly when food is withheld and the CS is given by itself. Why is this? In Pavlov's theorizing, it was suggested that a direct connection between the CS and UCS was formed in the brain during acquisition; it would therefore be simplest to assume that the same connection was gradually destroyed in extinction – the period when the CR slowly disappears. But 'spontaneous recovery' of the CR, after a period of rest (as shown in Fig. 3.1) proves that some association between the CS and UCS has remained intact despite the waning of the response in extinction. Pavlov's explanation was that the original association was not broken, but somehow pushed to one side by a process of *inhibition*. The details of this process are obscure, but the 'inhibition' concept has proved useful for dealing with the suppression of conditioned responses in extinction; they are apparently never completely forgotten.

Discrimination and generalization. The inhibition concept also comes in useful for interpreting the effects of stimuli which become signals for 'no food'. If a buzzer is used as the signal for food, a dog will salivate for a sound that bears almost any resemblance to the buzzer, although the amount of salivation will be less and less for sounds that are more and more unlike the proper signal. This responsiveness to stimuli because of their similarity to a CS is called *stimulus generalization*. However, dogs can make extremely fine auditory discriminations with the benefit of experience, as is evident from the habit, seen in many household pets, of anticipating the arrival of a familiar person on the basis of footsteps, or even car noises. Obviously when such a fine discrimination has been established, stimulus generalization has been drastically reduced.

Pavlov's experimental study of discrimination was accomplished by presenting positive and negative conditioned stimuli to the same animal. The positive CS signals food, but the negative CS signals 'no food'. With enough experience of these circumstances, a dog may become conditioned to salivate to the positive CS, but not to the negative CS. This kind of discrimination may be demonstrated using only two stimuli, such as a high-pitched and a low-pitched tone: if only the high-pitched tone is followed by food, the dog learns to salivate only to the high-pitched tone, and not to the low tone. Pavlov also used some rather complicated combinations and sequences of stimuli to demonstrate the inhibitory properties of a 'no food' signal. He gives one example of a dog first trained with three separate positive signals: a flashing light, a tone of C sharp, and a rotating disc. All these were signals for food and made the dog salivate. Then an 'inhibitory combination' was formed by sounding a metronome along with the rotating disc, and not giving food with this combination so that the dog learned not to salivate when the metronome tick and rotation occurred together. Now the inhibitory effects of the metronome could be tested by sounding it along with the other positive signals of the tone or the flashing light. When this was done the usual salivation produced by the positive signals was virtually eliminated. Having taken the precaution of showing that the metronome would not suppress salivation before it was used as a 'no-food' signal, Pavlov felt justified in concluding that the metronome had become a *conditioned inhibitor*. In other words, some stimuli which do not provoke a conditioned response are not neutral, but are signals for suppressing the response. This notion is common in theories of discrimination learning, which are discussed in more detail in Chapter 8.

Conditioning and the biological clock. Although very definite stimuli such as buzzers and light flashes are used for most experimental purposes, conditioning may take place with much more subtle signal sources. One internal signal source which is very indefinite, but seems to work accurately, is the 'biological clock' – a name given to some mechanism which is presumed to allow judgement of time without external clocks. Dogs fed on the hour every hour will salivate 'on time' if a feeding is missed out, and time intervals are involved in the delay- and trace-conditioning forms of the Pavlovian procedure. In *delay-conditioning* the CS starts several minutes before the food is due, instead of the usual few seconds, and continues until the UCS (food) is delivered. *Trace-conditioning* is similar except that the CS is turned off some time before the UCS appears. In both cases sufficient training results in the 'timing' of the CR so that most salivation occurs just before food is due. This suggests that the conditioned stimuli may initiate timing processes which in turn produce the conditioned responses.

Conditioned conditioned stimuli. A very strong CS, that is, one which reliably leads to much salivation, can be used instead of food to induce salivation in response to a new cue, which therefore is never actually paired with food. This is not very easily done, but Pavlov quotes a successful case where salivation was first conditioned to a buzzer. A black square was then held in front of the dog for ten seconds and followed after a break by the buzzer. After ten of these pairings the dog salivated a small but significant amount at the sight of the black square. Since food was never given in conjunction with the black square, steps had to be taken to prevent it becoming a 'no-food' signal and that is the reason for the break between the square and the buzzer. This type of *higher-order conditioning* has rarely been extended beyond the second order, but a long sequence of individual stimuli may be established, if there is always a reliable UCS at the end of it. Dogs given unpleasant injections very soon react at the sight of the syringe (Pavlov, 1927) and, equally, human activities which are advance preparations for going out for walks or providing food are not lost on dogs interested in the usual outcome of the preparations.

Backward conditioning. It is virtually impossible to obtain conditioned responses to a CS which begins after the onset of the UCS: if a dog is already eating, buzzers and lights tend to be ignored, and may not make the dog salivate if they are turned on without the food, even if they have accompanied eating and the after-eating period many times. It is hard to imagine why backward conditioning should be so difficult with stimuli which condition very easily if they are used as advance signals for food in the normal Pavlovian way. It may have something to do with the 'blocking' of attention to less important events once the more important UCS has started (see Ch. 8). Whatever the explanation, practically all experiments which have compared backward conditioning with the normal forward conditioning procedure have found backward conditioning much less effective for both animal and human subjects.

Words as signals. 'Speech provides stimuli which exceed in richness and many-sidedness any of the others, allowing comparison neither qualitatively or quantitatively with any conditioned stimuli which are possible in animals'. (Pavlov, 1927, p. 407.) Language is said to provide us with a *second signalling system* in which words can serve as substitutes for things (see Ch. 9). There are many different ways in which words can be interpreted as conditioned stimuli but Pavlov and Russian psychologists influenced by him have been particularly interested in the way in which words in the form of instructions can directly elicit human actions. An extreme case of this is seen in hypnotic suggestion, which interested Pavlov, but Luria (1961) has considerably refined the concept of speech as a method of eliciting behaviour by showing how susceptibility to instruction, and later the use of self-instruction, develops in young children. (See C2 and A7 for further information about cognitive development and language.)

Conditioning processes and personality. Pavlov rapidly came to the conclusion that the dogs which took part in his experiments could be classified into personality types. At first he chose dogs that were very lively and friendly, only to find that these animals went to sleep during the experiments at the first hint of monotony. When dogs who were generally shy, nervous and quiet were tested, they turned out to be more convenient, in so far as they stayed awake during even the most tedious experimental routines, and made very reliable and precise conditioned responses. It looked as though there were two definite personality types: 'The first needs a continuous and novel succession of stimuli, which may indeed be absent in the natural surroundings; the other, on the contrary, needs extremely uniform conditions of life.' (Pavlov, 1927, p. 287.)

These categories correspond to the classical sanguine or phlegmatic types, or the modern distinction between extrovert and introvert, which is to some extent based on Pavlov's ideas (Eysenck, 1973).

Another dimension of personality is resistance to stress, or stability, versus neuroticism. A kind of neurotic breakdown in general behaviour can be observed in animals in two kinds of situation: first if they are exposed to extremely intense or unpleasant stimuli, and second if they are in a situation of unresolvable conflict between alternative responses. Examples of these two stresses given by Pavlov were the major flood in Leningrad in 1924 which had traumatic effects on the 'inhibitable' dogs, and an experimental procedure which produced conflict by using a circle as a correct signal and an ellipse as an incorrect signal, with the ellipse being made rounder and rounder until it was extremely difficult to distinguish the ellipse from the circle. Some dogs were able to cope with stresses of these kinds, but others became over-excitable, with excessive barking, and biting of leads (these would be the neurotic extrovert type); still others became very withdrawn and unresponsive and lost weight (the 'inhibitable' or neurotic introvert type). Modern research (see D3) is directed towards the question of how far characterization of human personality, based on questionnaire answers or clinical description, can be related to variables such as arousal level (see Ch. 2) and conditionability.

Conditioning and counter-conditioning of human emotions

For a recent conditioning experiment, young men in Australia were asked to watch a travelogue film about London. They must have been well aware that the film might be slightly unusual, since they had agreed to have measuring devices attached to their penises while it was being shown to them. They were not disappointed in this expectation, since the travel film was interrupted every minute or so and replaced by ten seconds of a film showing an attractive and naked lady. It was intended that the lady should be associated not with views of London, but with an arbitrary conditioned stimulus, a red circle, which signalled the brief episodes in which she appeared. The exact form taken by interruptions of the travel film was that the red circle appeared for ten seconds and was immediately followed by ten seconds of the nude female figure.

The results of this experiment (Barr and McConaghy, 1972) clearly showed the classical conditioning of sexual arousal. First of all there was an unconditioned response (UCR): practically all the subjects had some degree of penile erection during the nude scenes (even small changes in the state of the penis can be accurately recorded with appropriate measuring devices). But by the time the red circle had preceded the nude scene on five or six occasions penile erection also occurred during the red circle presentations. In Pavlovian terms the red circle was now a conditioned stimulus for sexual arousal.

In a similar experiment an artificial fascination with footwear was induced in male volunteers by showing slides of black knee-length boots just before slides of nude females. Apart from acquiring physiological responses to pictures of the boots, the subjects reported that the boots aroused sexual ideas and feelings, which generalized to other kinds of boots, black shoes, and in one case even to sandals (Rachman and Hodgson, 1968).

Such results add support to the suggestion that many human emotional states become identified with triggering situations through processes akin to classical conditioning. Other factors are undoubtedly involved in normal (and abnormal) emotional development, but the classical conditioning procedure supplies a relatively straightforward technique for attempting to alter emotional attitudes to particular stimuli in the course of therapy.

Aversion therapy is a method used in attempts to establish a negative emotional reaction to stimuli judged to have too strong a positive attraction – mainly in cases of alcoholism or homosexuality (see F3). It consists of the Pavlovian procedure of pairing unpleasant events, usually electric shocks or drug-induced nausea, with the target situation, though opinions vary as to whether additional elaborations of the basic pairing are necessary. A method like this is hardly a satisfactory solution to the problems that may be raised by alcoholism or homosexuality, and could be made unnecessary by alternative approaches to treatment. But it has provided some respite from unwanted impulses for people who desired it, and continues to be used occasionally for this reason. For instance, Marks, *et al.* (1970) reported that a reduction in the unwanted activities and fantasies of male transvestites, fetishists and sadomasochists, produced by an aversion treatment, lasted throughout the follow-up period of two years. The treatment had relied on pairing electric shocks with both overt behaviours (e.g. dressing in women's clothes) and fantasies during a two-week stay in hospital. They also reported however that similar treatment had no long-term effect on patients who wished to change their sex.

A more indirect way of altering sexual impulses involves using slides or films as conditioned stimuli, as in the experiments above. A considerable amount of data suggests that the attractiveness of homosexual activities can be reduced by this means. The procedure is to use slides of men, which are initially sexually arousing to the patient, as signals for electric shocks. It is not surprising, perhaps, that the slides lose their attractiveness, but it is rather unexpected that the process generalizes to homosexual fantasies and activities outside treatment sessions, so that these too may become less attractive.

Aversion therapy has been used more frequently with alcoholics than with any other category of patient. In follow-up studies to evaluate the effects of aversion treatments for alcoholics, it is generally found that about half of those treated abstain from drinking for at least a year afterwards. That does not sound very promising, but this relapse rate compares favourably with other forms of treatment. With no treatment at all it is very rare for alcoholics to give up drinking or return to normal drinking (Meyer and Chesser, 1970).

Counter-conditioning to remove anxiety. It is widely believed that anxieties and fears may result from previous unpleasant or tragic experiences, which is consistent with explanations in terms of conditioning. A well-known experiment by Watson and Rayner (1920) demonstrated the conditioning of a fear in 'Little Albert', an eleven-month placid child who initially showed a fondness for white rats. This fondness was quickly replaced by fear after the sight of the white rat had been followed on six occasions by the loud crash of a steel bar being hammered. The fear was still apparent when Albert was tested five days later, and generalized without further conditioning trials to a white rabbit and a seal-skin coat which had previously caused no alarm. But if fears and anxieties have been conditioned-in, can they be conditioned-out? The finding of spontaneous recovery after extinction, referred to earlier, suggests that some remnant of any conditioning experience persists even if the conditioned response lapses. However, I have already described in the last chapter how some forms of behaviour therapy manage to reduce anxiety simply by exposing patients to the anxiety-provoking stimulus in an altered form; either progressive changes in a tolerable version of the stimulus (desensitization) or confrontation with an extreme form (flooding). More often than not, though, in these kinds of therapy, an attempt is made actively to condition-in a new response to replace and counteract anxiety. There are many physical and emotional responses which serve as distractions or comforts in the face of worry or agitation: whistling, singing, talking, smoking, eating, drinking, pacing up and down. But of course the effect of these is usually temporary, and in many cases excessive eating, drinking or smoking related to anxiety constitutes a problem in itself.

Deep muscular relaxation on the other hand has few unwanted side effects and is used almost universally when an anxiety-reducing response is needed in desensitization therapy. Patients are usually trained to relax by practice in alternately tensing and relaxing different muscle groups, although hypnosis or tranquillizers are sometimes included to assist training, and occasionally as a substitute for voluntary relaxation. Once a reliable procedure for relaxation has been established, the goal is to make relaxation the CR to stimuli that formerly caused anxiety and tension. In theory, this requires that the anxiety-provoking stimulus is used as a CS which signals a state of relaxation. In practice, it is found sufficient that patients maintain a state of relaxation while imagining progressively 'worse' situations, and it seems as though the relaxation allows the patient to get used to, or habitate to, the feared stimulus. As with most methods of therapy, there is some disagreement about exactly why desensitization works, and there are probably several reasons for its success. The 'counter-conditioning' principle is more directly visible in therapy where a more active response is trained to replace anxiety. In assertion training and some forms of sex therapy it is more obvious that assertive behaviours are being used to replace anxiety associated with shyness, or sexual behaviours used to replace anxiety to do with sex (F3).

Conclusion and summary

The laws of classical conditioning were established by measuring the secretion of dogs' salivary glands and can be seen to apply best with similar responses, that is responses which are involuntary or controlled by the autonomic nervous system. In particular this includes aspects of emotional reactions. In a wide sense, classical conditioning means that stimuli paired together in time become associated, responses given to one being also given to the other. Experimentally, one of the stimuli must precede the other, when they are paired, and the major effect is then that responses given to the second come to be made, in anticipation, to the first stimulus. If, subsequently, the leading stimulus occurs repeatedly by itself, the conditioned response dies away (extinction), but there is a residual effect which allows for spontaneous recovery. Speculation, supported by experiments with human subjects, suggests that previously-experienced associations govern human emotional reactions. Modifications to emotional reactions may be brought about in the course of therapy by using classical conditioning procedures, either by associating withdrawal from painful stimuli with impulses to be suppressed, or by associating relaxation with stimuli which evoke undue anxiety.

4
Operant conditioning: reward and positive reinforcement

Operant conditioning has to do with reward and punishment, with achieving goals and avoiding disasters. In Skinner's terminology, goals, rewards and incentives may all be referred to as *positive reinforcers*; achieving the goal or receiving the reward is *positive reinforcement*. Escaping from unpleasant or dangerous situations is classified as *negative reinforcement*. Reinforcement is thus always the occasion for things becoming better than they were, but is divided up according to whether it is some new good thing which happens, or something bad which goes away. Punishment is distinguished from reinforcement because it is a moment when things get definitely worse, either through loss of positive reinforcers, as in fines or confiscations, or through the onset of an aversive state of affairs such as physical pain or social rejection.

The lynch-pin of the Skinnerian system (see Ch. 1) is positive reinforcement, which allows behaviour to be changed by the influence of attractive consequences. Both negative reinforcement and punishment involve some degree of *aversive control*, which is the use of unpleasant stimuli to modify behaviour, and they will be left to the next chapter.

Positive reinforcement is of interest for two separate reasons; first as one of the most powerful techniques we have at our disposal for directing or motivating the actions of other people or animals, either in the laboratory or in the outside world. The second reason is almost a philosophical one; the versatility of the *concept* of reinforcement as an explanation of behaviour. The answer to the question 'why do people behave as they do?' can often be given in the form 'because they are reinforced for it'. People can be said to work for the reinforcers for working, and play because of the reinforcers for playing. The main advantage of giving a preliminary answer in this way is that it prompts the further question 'what *are* the reinforcers?' in any particular case, and this may be something which can be determined by the traditional scientific means of observation and experiment. It remains to be seen how far this explanatory use of the positive reinforcement concept can be justified, but Skinner (1953) has given analyses of almost every area of human activity. The reinforcement idea has recently been taken up in both clinical and social psychology (F3, B1) but the original examples of carefully measured operant conditioning came from the animal laboratory.

Operant learning in various forms

Whenever rewards are given or behaviours change according to their usefulness, the essential features of positive reinforcement are present. Operant learning therefore takes in a very broad sweep of circumstances in which separate areas have their own special characteristics. A brief survey of several kinds of training or experience in which positive reinforcement plays a part is given below.

Shaping operant responses by successive approximation

Figure 4.1 illustrates the arrangement used by Ferster and Skinner (1957) in their extensive research on positive reinforcement (see Ch. 6). The reinforcer is food, given to a hungry animal. This is by far the most frequently employed incentive in animal experiments since it is convenient, harmless and very effective. However there is nowadays a greater interest in studying a variety of reinforcers to see which works best for a particular response (Hinde and Stevenson-Hinde, 1973). A number of rewards have been explored, including access to the opposite sex, opportunities for exercise and the delivery of bits of paper to make nests with (see Ch. 7). Returning to the apparatus in Figure 4.1, the all-important reinforcer is in this case the availability of grain for a few seconds

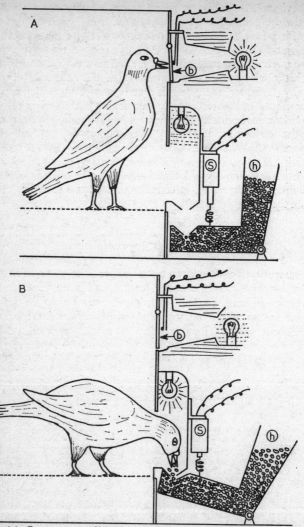

Fig. 4.1 *Operant conditioning apparatus for pigeons.* In A the bird has just made contact with the pecking button (*b*). In B this peck is reinforced: current is supplied to a solenoid (*s*) which lifts up the grain hopper (*h*) for a few seconds. (After Ferster and Skinner, 1957)

at a time, when a food-hopper is brought within a pigeon's reach.

As a prerequisite for any response shaping the subject must be adapted to the experimental situation and become accustomed to eating out of the food magazine (*magazine training*). A hungry bird soon becomes adept at recovering grain as fast as possible while it is presented. By this point, if food is available for only three seconds out of every minute, the pigeon will waste no time getting down to eat the food as soon as food is signalled by the sound of the mechanism and the lighting up of the hopper. The sound and light are said to have become *discriminative stimuli* for getting to the hopper and eating. Now the very strong influence of food delivery on the pigeon's behaviour patterns can be demonstrated. The most commonly studied response of the bird in this context is that of directing a strong peck towards a flat recessed button on the wall. This records the response automatically and delivers the reinforcer. To persuade the pigeon to make this response by successive approximation an experimenter must watch the bird carefully, and make a series of decisions about what the bird must do to earn a few seconds access to food. To start with, the experimenter might deliver food (by pushing his own button to activate the mechanism) if the bird raised its head to within a few inches of the pecking button. This usually has a quite dramatic effect, the bird quickly returning to the posture required by the time four or five reinforcements have been given. Now the experimenter might wait until the pigeon makes a movement towards the pecking button before delivering food. This results in the bird repeating the movement, and then the criterion for reward can be made closer and closer to a real peck. Sooner or later the bird succeeds in operating the pecking button itself, and it can then be left to feed itself automatically, if it gains a small amount of food every time it pecks the button.

Although, as outlined in the next section, any form of pecking is an easy response to shape in birds, the value of the response-shaping method is that it can be used to induce a wide variety of behaviour patterns, provided the reinforcer is powerful enough, and progress is made gradually. Shaping is a major tool in the training of handicapped or retarded people by operant methods, especially in combination with some form of prompting (see below). It is especially appropriate as a method of teaching when other forms of communication are impossible. I recently saw shaping being used to teach a severely retarded blind child to operate his wheel chair. A spoon of icecream was held just in front of his mouth as he sat in the chair, so that a slight movement of his hands to turn the wheels of his chair forward was reinforced by contact with the icecream. After starting off with the criterion that just the placing of his hands on the wheels was rewarded by giving icecream, greater and greater success in moving the chair was needed as the icecream was held further and further away. This is an example of how positive reinforcement can provide both information and incentive at the same time. Getting icecream and social approval can be an encouragement for the task, and at the same time the prompt delivery of positive reinforcers supplies information about the correctness of target responses in a way that resembles *feedback* (see A5) for response skills.

Autoshaping, prompting and guidance
The gradual-shaping procedure can sometimes work quickly, but often requires a good deal of patience and skill on the part of the shaper. He must wait for the subject to make the appropriate response, but must also make sure that enough rewards are given to maintain interest. Measures to get the correct response without prolonged shaping have always been sought; rats may be attracted by cheese smeared on a lever and there are several short-cuts for training pigeons (Ferster and Skinner, 1957).

Autoshaping. Another method of ensuring that animals come up with a response has been devised by Brown and Jenkins (1968). The general idea is to attract attention to a stimulus source by using it as a signal for food, and to wait until the subject makes some kind of response *directed at* the stimulus source. With pigeons, it is sufficient to light-up the pecking button for a few seconds before the grain hopper operates. As we would expect from classical conditioning experiments (see p. 36), the birds cannot remain indifferent to a stimulus that signals food, and after about fifty trials (fifty pairings of the light signal with the reinforcer, with an average of a minute or so between pairings) they peck at the light sufficiently strongly to operate the button. If operating the button pays off with immediate food delivery this will strengthen the tendency to respond, but even if there is no pay-off for responding, the tendency to peck at the food signal is pronounced. This *auto-shaping* procedure is a mixture of stimulus-learning (classical conditioning) and response shaping (operant conditioning) which makes use of the investigative responses of the subject (Jenkins, 1973). Thus subjects can be lured to a particular location by a light source that signals reward, and this acts as a form of response shaping. Pigeons peck at the signal source, rats and dogs poke at it with their nose or paw, and monkeys or people may grab it with their hands.

Prompting and guidance. Autoshaping can be viewed as a form of *prompting*, which is a term used liberally for a number of additional techniques of facilitating a certain activity including even physically pushing and pulling the subject through the required movements (which can also be referred to as *guidance* or *putting through*). Many operant training procedures are combinations of shaping by approximation with a variety of prompts. For instance a combination was used to inculcate the social behaviour of greetings in some children in a home for the retarded (Stokes, Baer and Jackson, 1974). The positive reinforcers were candies, potato crisps and the social rewards of a smile and a pat on the head. The goal was to get some rather withdrawn boys to smile, wave and if possible say hello when they met someone; improvements in such basic social skills often reap additional benefits in social adjustment and interaction. Initially, a very low response criterion and physical prompts were necessary. The experimenter greeted the boy, and in the absence of any spontaneous reaction, gently pulled the boy's arm back and forth in a crude waving motion, as a *physical prompt*, before giving some crisps or sweets. After some training like this, a *visual prompt* was added to assist the learning of a freer 'wave': sweets were waved to and fro slowly, followed by the subject's hand, before they were delivered, along with social approval and encouragement. Gradually more realistic greeting responses were required, and the final stage of training was to employ a different training person, with the emphasis on social reinforcers, so that the greeting behaviour generalized to normal meetings with other people in day-to-day interactions.

Prompts which require some degree of comprehension by the subject include imitative prompts, or 'showing how', and instructions of the form 'do this' or 'do that' (see Ch. 9). If ordinary instructions and explanations are sufficient to determine future behaviour patterns, there is of course no need for special training procedures. But for most skills practice is necessary even if detailed verbal advice is available (you can be 'told how' to ride a bicycle without much benefit). And teachers and parents soon find out that instructions which sound easy enough may require some motivational emphasis if they are to be followed. Combinations of instructions and positive reinforcement are often called for because of these factors, but are always prominent when the normal course of educational or social inducements has proved inadequate. Allyon and Azrin (1964) found a case where neither instructions nor a simple increase in positive reinforcement worked to bring about a change in behaviour. Mental patients had lost the habit of picking-up their cutlery in a ward dining-room run on the cafeteria system. Offering 'extras' (additional cigarettes, cups of coffee etc) when patients remembered their cutlery, without explanation, did not make any difference. Reminding the patients ('please pick up your knife, fork and spoon') at each meal helped at first, but the effect was short-lived. However, giving verbal reminders plus rewards for successful behaviour led to almost complete recovery, in all twenty patients involved, of the expedient of collecting their cutlery. Since they used the cutlery when they were in possession of it, but tried to manage without cutlery if they had forgotten it, the extra training improved general dining behaviour considerably.

Often when prompts are used in initial training, the final goal will require the subject to act without help from this source. Leaving out prompts so that the subject responds on his own, or *fading*, is one aspect of the gradual shaping method. It has to be done with care because too much prompting may produce an awkward dependence on the prompts, and fast removal of the prompts may make the task to difficult. For instance, children may be helped to use spoons by an adult holding the spoon as well, and doing most of the work to start with. Especially with handicapped children, there may have to be very gradual fading of this prompt, so that the child does eventually learn to feed himself, but does not give up along the way.

Schedules of reinforcement

A tremendous amount of work has been done on the effects of

schedules of reinforcement on animal behaviour. The experiments are usually controlled automatically (nowadays by a computer) and the schedule of reinforcement is the automatic rule about when positive reinforcers are delivered. Obviously simple rules or *schedules* have been studied most. The simplest schedule of all is that where a single behaviour is measured, and every response gets a reinforcer. In Skinner's original experiment, a food pellet was dropped into a bowl for a rat to eat every time the rat pressed down a bar. This is called fixed ratio 1 (FR 1) or continuous reinforcement (CRF). For fixed ratio 2 every second response brings down the food pellet, for fixed ratio 3 every third response, and so on. All these are *fixed ratio schedules*, in which there is an exact relationship between the number of responses made and the number of rewards given. Spacing out the reinforcers without requiring very much behaviour can be done with *fixed interval schedules*. Here only one response is actually needed to get the reinforcer, but responses don't work until a certain length of time has passed since the last reward. Usually what happens is that animals do not wait until reward is obtainable, but respond during the interval until the reinforcer is delivered. On fixed interval (FI) schedules the interval is the same every time, and animals learn to respond more vigorously as reward becomes due. To produce a steadier rate of response the intervals can be made of unpredictable length so that animals learn to bash away at their response very regularly, because the reinforcer might become available at any moment. With these unpredictable intervals, the procedure is called a *variable interval schedule*. It is often employed to ensure a stable behavioural *baseline*. Less often used, because training with it is more difficult, is the variable version of the fixed ratio, the *variable ratio schedule*.

Note that in these intermittent schedules of reinforcement reinforcers do not have to be given for every response.

Response skills

It is often possible in everyday situations to distinguish between the motives for attempting a task, and the factors which allow for mastery of it. In many competitive sports for instance, the reinforcers for engaging in them may have to do with the excitement of the competition, the joys of winning, or the social fringe benefits, whereas the learning and preparation for taking part may involve many hours of tedious, painful or lonely practice. The reinforcers for acquiring a skill need not be the same as those obtained by exercising it. Rewards given for success may be sufficient for inducing further effort without supplying a noticable increase in proficiency: no amount of celebration surrounding the achievement by a golfer of a hole-in-one is likely to improve his swing, although it may encourage him to spend much more time playing. On the other hand the swing may be improved by certain prompts, such as criticism of style, changes of grip and so on, which are not much fun in themselves. (See A5.)

In some cases, however, the immediate effect of responses is the single most important factor in the further development of skill, including cases where the main result of a response is to produce a positive reinforcer. *Response differentiation* by selective reinforcement is an example of this.

Response differentiation. The lever-pressing apparatus for rats provides a method for studying the learning of precision movements. A rat may press down the lever with one or other of its paws, or its mouth, from various angles or positions. These are called variations in response topography. Easier to measure are the quantitive aspects of lever movement, such as the exact force exerted or distance moved which are normally pretty unpredictable.

Both response topography, and quantitative features of lever pressing, may be refined by selective reinforcement. Very fine response differentiations can be recorded when quantitative methods are used. Rats may be conditioned to press down the lever to a certain angle, or to press with a certain force, or for a certain duration.

Biofeedback. It is generally true that selective reinforcement will encourage behaviour in the required range and that these tasks are made much easier by appropriate external feedback. The enhancement of behaviour by external feedback is nowhere more evident than in control of biological functions by the method known as *biofeedback* (see A2), which seems to enable a degree of voluntary control over the activity of internal organs. It is not normally sufficient merely to try to bring about a particular rate of heart beat, or a particular state of the brain which produces the 'alpha rhythm' form of brainwaves. This is partly because it is difficult to know when success has been achieved, and there can be no reinforcement or feedback from good responses. A remedy has been found in the electrical measurement of the target biological function, and the provision of a clear external signal for success and failure. Such 'bio-feed-back machines' are now commercially available as shortcuts to meditation or relaxation. Of course connecting up some-one to one of these machines will not produce a state of meditation unless he makes an effort to produce the correct signal, that is unless the correct signal acts as a reinforcer. After being connected up one must follow the instructions to try and 'make the needle stay on the right' or 'try and produce the low pitched tones' and this takes some practice.

When trying to relax, it may help to 'make the mind go blank' or concentrate on a peaceful image, while lying or sitting in calming positions. When trying to increase arousal it is pos-sible to change breathing patterns, tense muscles, imagine night-marish situations.

Would biofeedback work without any of these stratagems? Attempts were made to answer this question by doing experi-ments on rats temporarily paralysed by a curare-like drug, and artificially respirated, in the hope of finding results not due to muscle movements made by the animals. Such internal activi-ties as intestinal contractions and heart-rate increases or de-creases were selectively reinforced by electrical brain stimulation (see A2 and Ch. 7). The original results from such experiments suggested a high degree of direct control of such functions by electrical brain stimulation, which was assumed to have com-bined feedback and reinforcing functions. But further experi-mentation has modified the initial conclusions somewhat, since the effect is not as powerful as was first thought. The effect is indirect because it depends on previous experiences of the ani-mals before they were paralysed (Miller and Dworkin, 1974). Current opinion supports the conclusion that biofeedback works indirectly, by allowing for reinforcement of any response strate-gem or internal activity which helps produce the target be-haviour. This type of reinforcement can assist in behavioural therapy for physical symptoms, as in the re-training of abnormal heart rhythms in cardiac patients (Brener, 1973). Patients are trained to produce normal heart rhythms with external feed-back and the feedback is then faded out (in the same way that prompts are gradually removed) so that more normal heart functioning is maintained outside the training laboratory.

Response timing. Correct timing of responses is an important part of most skills and the direct reinforcement of responses made at certain intervals has been much investigated in the operant conditioning apparatus. A procedure called the *differential reinforcement of low rates* (DRL) ensures that responses are spaced apart in time. If responses are made too frequently no rewards are given, but any response made at the correct time after the previous one (fifteen seconds for example) delivers the reinforcer. Very elaborate sequences of accurately-timed responses can be observed. It is possible that internal timing of responses is the explanation for many of the effects of intermittent reinforcement schedules (Blackman, 1974, and Ch. 6).

Spatial learning: finding food and finding out
Testing the ability of animals to find their way through mazes is a well-tried form of psychological experiment. In their natural environment many animals exhibit astounding navigational abilities (like the return of salmon to their native streams and the 'homing' of pigeons). Most laboratory feats are much less impressive, but provide the basis for quantitative study.

Alley running. Although rats should be good at remembering where food is, it actually takes them a considerable amount of time to reach a final level of performance in a task as simple as running from one end of a straight alley to another to get to food. It might take twenty or thirty trials before the rat runs down the alley at its maximum speed (three or four feet per second), although the most rapid change in behaviour would take place over the first five or ten trials. If food is left out of the goal box (*extinction*: Ch. 6) there would again be a fairly rapid change in the first ten experiences; this time a slowing down, which would continue for many more trials before reaching a stable level. One concept clearly illustrated by alley-running is that of *incentive*, which corresponds roughly to the degree of enthusiasm attached to reinforced behaviours. In alley-running this is expressed as speed. In subjective terms this eagerness might be a product of an expectation of or hope for the reward, but in the practicalities of the experiment it simply reflects the tastiness or size of the rewards previously given. Rats given minute amounts of food in the goal box will increase their speed of running towards the goal very gradually, and will never bother to run very fast. Rats given large tasty portions at the end of their run react a great deal more energetically. In Hullian theory (see D2 and Ch. 1) this effect of *amount* of reinforcement was referred to as *incentive motivation*; nowadays any effect on the vigour or energy of reinforced behaviour due to the quality or quantity of reinforcers is conveniently put in the incentive category. This view of incentive as an emotional anticipation of reinforcement is supported by rapid changes in mood apparently produced by changing the amount of reward given. If training takes place with a large reward, switching to a medium reward has a depressing effect, whereas with some training routines, switching to a medium reward after training with a very small reinforcer produces an extra degree of incentive (Crespi, 1942). Another factor which moderates enthusiasm in alley-running is the *delay of reward*. If the animal has to wait at the end of the run for some time before food is dropped in, its speed of running diminishes. In the response-shaping technique it is usually valuable to give reinforcers as soon as possible after the target response, in case some other behaviour intervenes and the reward is wasted. But even if reward is contingent on the correct response it is obvious that having to wait for the reinforcer will decrease its incentive value.

Choice and cognition in mazes. The element of choice can be included in the running task by releasing a laboratory animal from the bottom end of a T-shaped maze with food at only one of the ends of the cross bar. If sufficient geographical information is available in the form of landmarks – recognizable objects and constant sources of light or smells – rats will learn the food is 'over there' rather than remembering any particular route to get to the food, although details of route are important in more complex mazes of the Hampton Court type. That the form rather than the substance of a maze problem can be remembered is shown by the ability of rats to swim through a maze which they have learned by walking. In the early stages of learning rats are hesitant about making a decision at a *choice-point*, where they can go either left or right. They have a marked tendency to make one or two steps in one direction, give a couple of sniffs, and then withdraw back to their original position. Tolman dubbed this behaviour *vicarious trial and error* as it seems to consist of a small scale testing out of the choices of turning left or right. It emphasizes the fact that positive reinforcement may produce dilemmas and that choice between two activities that have equal incentive may be difficult. Rats have more difficulty learning a T-maze when there are four pellets of food on the left and three pellets on the right, than when the choice is between four and zero. Thus, although knowing where we are is mainly a function of the familiarity of the ground, and 'cognitive maps' of geographical information can be built up in the absence of specific goals, it is the importance, or incentive value of specific goals which most influences decisions about which way to turn next.

Creative responses

One of the limitations of the shaping procedure as an educational technique is that the learner does only what he is trained to do, which might not inculcate the valuable qualities of imagination and initiative. It is often held that positive reinforcement is an inherently narrowing influence on behaviour, and cannot assist in developing intelligent or original responses. This narrowing aspect of operant learning is almost certainly a matter of the uses to which positive reinforcement is normally put, rather than an inherent limitation. There is certainly no reason why prizes cannot be given for originality to give incentive for creativity, or why teachers and parents should not give approval for novel activities. If originality does not result, this may be because of the inherent difficulty of the task, rather than the ineffectiveness of the encouragement. Provided the demands made are not too great, it is possible to use reinforcement procedures to train a subject to make a *different* response, rather than to make the *same* response. Not much inventiveness is usually expected of rats, but it is easy enough for them to learn to press a different lever than the last, instead of the same lever as the last, when they have the choice of two (Foster *et al.*, 1970).

Actual invention of new acrobatic tricks seems to have been achieved by porpoises trained to produce novel responses (Pryor *et al.*, 1969). With one porpoise, the plan was not to induce originality, but simply to shape-up a new trick (selected by the trainer) every day for the purpose of public demonstration. A reward of fish signalled by a whistle was given for successive approximations to the desired trick. However, after several days of this the animal pre-empted shaping by coming up with 'an unprecedented range of behaviours' off her own bat. The effect was repeated for thirty-two sessions with a second porpoise, until the novel patterns of aerial movement achieved by the subject became too complex for objective description.

The result suggests that, at least for porpoises, 'novelty' may be reinforced. Another way of putting this is to say that a *class* of behaviour may be subjected to the training procedure. The class that is specified by stating that behaviour each day must be novel is probably very difficult initially, because the non-reinforcement of previously 'good' behaviour is frustrating. But once the response class has been established, or the principle learned, this problem is not so important.

Generative response classes and response generalization

A frequent objection to the idea that positive reinforcement applies to human behaviours has been that external rewards and punishments do not seem to explain those many areas of human accomplishment where *rules* appear to be of greater importance than specific items of conduct. It is obvious that we are able to learn response classes such as 'being polite' and 'being aggressive', as well as 'being original', which may reveal themselves in unaccustomed circumstances. More fuss has been made about the business of rules from the point of view of linguistic analyses of speech than in other areas (see A7 and Ch. 9) and the term *generative response class* has arisen from this. If the reinforcement of a limited number of specific responses appears to be sufficient to establish the pattern of making similar responses in different, but appropriate, situations, a generative response class has been learned. This is distinct from having 'learned the rule', in that we (as well as animals) may be able to perform generative response classes without being able to say what the rule is. Conversely, we may 'know the rules' without being able to play, in the sense of being able to recite the principles of how to land a lunar module, or make the perfect tennis backhand, with no personal proficiency at these performances.

Several experiments have made it clear that the formation of generative response classes in verbal behaviour may be assisted by positive reinforcement. External reinforcers may not be critical during language development in infants (see C2 and Ch. 9) but can be used for experimental or remedial purposes. A major yardstick of fluency is the number of words strung together; babies start off with one-word utterances and take some time to develop long sentences. Grammatical rules or generative response classes include getting words in the right order, and adjusting the endings of words to fit in with the rest of what is being said (see A7, C2 and Ch. 9). One of the easiest rules about word-endings, in English, is putting an 's' on the end of plural nouns. Most children get used to this very soon, and will apply the rule to new words, sometimes incorrectly, as in 'mouses'. However, a child who does not say plurals properly can be helped to learn this response class by extra rewards for correct individual cases. After being praised, and given bites of food just after saying 'horses', 'cars' and 'shoes' when shown collections of these objects, a child may be better able to give the correct response when shown buses, dogs or hats, provided of course that he knows the correct singular term.

This kind of training for an eight-year-old autistic boy was described recently by Stevens-Long and Rasmussen (1974). The boy was given food and praise for using plurals correctly when he was asked to describe pictures. Imitative prompts (giving examples of proper kinds of phrase) and disapproval for errors, were also incorporated in the training programme and the same programme was continued to promote longer descriptions in the form of compound sentences. Similar teaching methods were effective with retarded children and normal toddlers who had not developed their speech to the target level when Lutzker and Shermna (1974) studied the learning of certain kinds of subject-verb agreement with these kinds of pupil. Rewards produced a very rapid improvement in the ability of the toddlers, as well as the retarded children, for giving descriptions of the type 'boats are sailing', instead of, for instance, 'boats is sailing'. The generative aspect of this response class lies in the facility for giving the correct kind of phrase to *new* pictures after the reward training. In other words, having been rewarded for saying 'boats are sailing' correctly puts the child on the right lines when it comes to a new description like 'girls are riding', even if no reinforcement has actually been given for phrases about girls or about riding. Often, however, a wide range of examples has to be used before the child being taught 'catches on' to the response class.

For adults as well as children positive reinforcement, especially in the form of social approval, biases people towards adopting or discarding complex styles of speech or attitudes of mind (C2). These cannot easily be described or measured, but they can count as *response classes* as long as we can tell which kind of behaviour belongs in each response category. Many of these classes of response, like 'taking care' or 'keeping a stiff upper lip' may be learned on the basis of limited experience, to be brought into action later in totally different situations. At least that is the assumption behind the belief that character-building 'on the playing fields of Eton', or in other forms of schooling, has a lasting effect. A somewhat similar attempt to cultivate broad classes of response takes place in a form of therapy known as *assertion training*. In this, shy or nervous people become more confident after they have been prompted and encouraged to practise acting assertively, initially perhaps by playing make-believe roles and 'acting' in the theatrical sense in improvised scenes (see F3). Obviously if a shy person suddenly becomes very assertive we might talk of a 'personality change' but 'altered response-classes' more accurately expresses what is observed.

If training in one situation helps someone to cope with many similar problems it is often said that *transfer of training* has taken place (Ch. 8), or just that there is *response generalization*. This can apply even when the 'generative response' notion is unnecessary. If someone has been speaking loudly in a noisy factory and carries on talking loudly at home, we might refer to response generalization, and this would also be so for someone who learned to speak up in assertion training with plenty of carry-over to everyday circumstances. It is often hard to distinguish between response and stimulus generalization, and so it is common for all effects of training or therapy to be lumped together as *generalization*. It is also difficult to distinguish between the generalization of fairly peripheral response effects, like walking faster or speaking louder, and generative responses which involve a greater degree of abstraction. *Semantic generalization* is an in-between stage where, for instance, subjects who have been reinforced for saying 'beach' might occasionally say 'sea-shore' or 'sand' instead; the meaning or other associations of a word may be remembered rather than the word itself (A6). In most real-life situations all the different kinds of generalization may blend together, so the distinctions between them are not always important.

One very well-known study of positive reinforcement in 'client-centred' therapy made use of response categories which depended on the combined judgement of several clinical psychologists. Therapy sessions consisted of conversations between the therapist and a 'client'. Clinical judgement was the basis for analysing tape-recordings by classifying the therapist's statements according to whether they showed approval or disapproval of the patient. In the same way the patient's statements were sorted into nine different categories such as 'problem orientation', 'anxiety', 'negative feelings' and, most important, 'similarity to therapist' (Truax, 1966). The pattern of when the therapist gave sympathy and agreement correlated with the way the patient gradually changed during the sessions of therapy. The therapist gave most approval when the patient talked about himself sensibly, especially if he used a verbal style like the therapist's own. The end result was that the patient talked sensibly about himself more often, and acquired some of the therapist's ways of speaking. Truax's conclusion was therefore that positive reinforcement by the therapist caused helpful changes in the patient, measured as very broad classes of response. There has been a long debate between the therapist in Truax's investigation, Carl Rogers, and B. F. Skinner about whether it is accurate to describe client-centred therapy in terms of positive reinforcement. Both Rogers and his clients believe that the atmosphere of warmth and 'positive regard' (Rogers, 1955) supplied by the therapist allows the patient to improve without value judgements or specific instructions (see D3). Whatever reinforcement there is must therefore be informal and intuitive. But the degree to which the reinforcement concept can be adapted to deal with Rogerian therapy (Meyer and Chesser, 1970) illustrates both the flexibility of the concept and the way in which complex kinds of thought and feeling can be interpreted as response classes.

Conclusion and summary

The cornerstone of operant conditioning is the proposition that behaviour is strengthened by contingent rewards. This is positive reinforcement, which is most visible in the feats performed by laboratory animals rewarded with food. Gradual shaping of new skills or categories of response can be useful in many contexts, especially when combined with additional means of directing behaviour such as prompting or instruction. The motivating powers of reinforcement can supply incentive for many items of conduct and influence a wide range of decisions and choices.

5
Operant conditioning: negative reinforcement and punishment

Unfortunate as it may be, motivating stimuli are not universally enjoyable. Living under the influence of constant social approval, exerting ourselves only to achieve internally-rewarding feedback or attractive conditions in the environment, would be all very well. As it is most of us spend some of the time working to wipe out debts, putting on extra clothes to stop feeling cold, moving the car to avoid getting a parking ticket, trying to get to meetings on time to avoid social disapproval, drinking to stave off anxiety and so on. In cases like these we are trying to minimize contact with aversive stimuli, rather than to achieve positive goals. Many aversive situations can be construed as a lack of a positive factor: being cold is the opposite of being warm, social rejection is the other side of the coin to social approval and so on. But unpleasant or frightening stimuli usually have some distinctive properties of their own, with particular behavioural repercussions. When cold we may shiver and when overheated sweat and pant; these extremes of discomfort precipitate actions directed towards escaping from the extremes rather than to bring about maximum comfort. Anxiety is more than the lack of happiness, and is clearly more than the lack of physical pleasure.

Negative reinforcers must therefore be considered as separate stimuli and motivators in their own right, not just as the absence of positive reinforcers. A negative reinforcer is defined as a stimulus which we would struggle to get away from, and escaping from a negative reinforcer is classified as *negative re-*

inforcement. Losing rewards and receiving pain are *punishers* in this scheme. There seems to be a strong natural tendency to think of punishment as being included under negative reinforcement, but the distinction between negative reinforcement and punishment is necessary. Negative reinforcement fosters the target response as a means of escape, whereas punishment as a rule deters or suppresses response.

Forms of learning with aversive stimuli

Behaviours are influenced by consequences, and this holds true by and large when the consequences are unpleasant. We normally lose enthusiasm for activities which bring about disasters and gain some facility for items of behaviour which alleviate pain or distress. There are, however, a number of special factors which enter into learning motivated by negative reinforcers. The disturbing emotional effects of aversive stimuli are susceptible to classical conditioning and this can alter the nature of the operant learning (see p. 66). There are side effects from the use of severely unpleasant reinforcers which bring stress, aggression and defensive reactions into the picture. Certain types of learning can be observed with few side-effects if mild negative reinforcers are employed, and these are discussed first.

Escape learning

Escape from confinement was one of the types of learning studied by Thorndike in 1898 (see Ch. 1). Putting cats inside a box proved sufficiently motivating to induce the gradual learning of a method of operating a latch which held the door. Since Thorndike many experimenters have employed electrical stimulation as a negative reinforcer for laboratory animals. This is most frequently delivered through metal bars on which the animals are standing, at levels which elicit escape movements but are not physically harmful. By this use of mild electric shocks, rats may be trained to press levers, or run through mazes, in much the same way as they can by using food as a positive reinforcer. Shaping can be used if the current is turned on every thirty seconds or so and turned off again when the animal makes an approximation to the desired response. Behaviour produced by such escape learning is often stereotyped, with less respite from the conditioned responses for exploration or grooming. For instance, when rats have to learn to press down a lever to escape from shock they tend to hold the lever down for long periods after the negative reinforcement of the shock going off. This by-product (rigidity in behaviour) is less pronounced however when weaker aversive circumstances, like loud noise or a draught of cold air, are the stimuli being turned off.

Avoidance learning

If animals are being trained to learn a T-maze (see p. 57) by negative reinforcement it is not necessary for the maze to be a continuously awful environment. Occasional electric shocks delivered in the body of the maze will be quite sufficient to motivate the animal to find a 'safe' compartment. In fact the avoidance of dangerous *places* is one of the strongest sequels to negative reinforcement. Extremely rapid learning can be observed, often as a result of a single experience, when painful stimuli are associated with a particular location. In the 'step-down test', for instance, a mouse is placed on a small 'safe' platform, above an electrified floor. Placing one foot on the electrified floor is usually enough to prevent any further moves from the platform for an extended period, which provides a crude measure of the animal's memory of the shock. It is obviously a good behavioural principle, on evolutionary grounds, for animals to avoid signs of danger and unfamiliar situations which are associated with pain (see p. 93). Very rapid learning is observed also when it is a matter of 'getting out' rather than 'staying put'. If rats are allowed to explore an enclosure for a time and are then shocked, they learn very quickly to jump up on to a 'safe' platform.

A special apparatus exploits the 'getting out' reaction to negative reinforcers by requiring animals to shuttle back and forth over a barrier, set at their shoulder height, between two compartments. Neither of the compartments is permanently safe, but only one is electrified at a time. The problem for the animal is therefore to find whichever side is safe. The usual procedure is to give a warning signal whenever the electrified side is to be changed, so that the animal can always avoid being shocked if he switches sides when he hears the warning signal. Most animals learn to avoid at least eight out of ten of the shocks by getting over the barrier in time, but the speed of learning is affected by many details of the procedure, and by the prior experience of the subjects. The idea is that emotional reactions to the painful stimulus are conditioned to the warning signal in accordance with the usual results of classical conditioning (p. 36). The anticipatory emotional reaction of fear or anxiety then serves as a negative reinforcer for any responses which reduce fear. This *two-factor theory* postulates that animals *first* learn to be afraid and *then* learn a response to reduce the fear. (Mowrer, 1960). In a demonstration of the two-factor theory Miller (1948) trained rats initially to run out of a white room, through a small door into a black room (of appropriate size), by giving shocks in the white room. After this pre-training, the door was closed, and could only be opened by the rats turning a wheel. Although no more shocks were given, the residual 'aversiveness' of the white room was sufficient for the rats quickly to learn to turn the wheel so that they could run through into the 'safe' room, thus relieving their anxiety.

Making sure prevents finding out. Miller's result is reminiscent of Tolman's experiments with food rewards, where positive incentive was attached to getting to a 'good' place where food was usually found, and rats would circumvent or climb over any new barriers along the route to the 'good' place. The 'conditioned negative reinforcer' of getting out of the white compartment into the black one is almost identical to the 'conditioned positive reinforcer' of getting to a black compartment that usually has food in it (see Ch. 7). But there is one crucial difference. If we try to persuade rats to learn new responses in order to get into a black box which *used* to have food in it, they will very soon stop bothering because they will learn that the black box no longer contains food. But if they are successfully escaping from a white room which *used* to be dangerous, they may go on indefinitely, because having escaped from the white room they cannot find out that it is no longer dangerous. This is a reason why actions motivated by conditioned fear or anxiety should persist longer than those influenced by positive incentives. Experiments with dogs and human subjects have shown that when strong stimuli are used to establish an avoidance response the response may continue indefinitely if it is not physically prevented (Solomon and Wynne, 1953; Turner and Solomon, 1962). If subjects are concerned enough to make sure that they avoid an anxiety-provoking situation, it will be very difficult to find out if the situation has changed. This is part of the learning theory analysis of the importance of anxiety in neurosis. If someone has a phobia about leaving the house *in case* something terrible happens, they may not leave the house for years, and this will simply make going out more frightening. The theory is that by going out without something terrible happening, or even imagining going out without anxiety, the conditioned avoidance response can be diminished (see F3, and Chs, 2 and 3).

Avoidance without fear. Solomon and Wynne trained their dogs to jump out of a compartment by giving a few strong shocks, and found that the dogs continued to jump out of the compartment for hundreds of trials without further shocks. There is little doubt that a state of conditioned anxiety elicited by the situation was responsible for this behaviour. Feelings of anxiety produced by car accidents, muggings, war experiences or childhood traumas may also persist for indefinite periods. But is it necessary that all avoidance behaviours should be accompanied by intense anxiety? Is it possible to make 'rational' avoidance responses, like taking an umbrella to avoid getting wet, without any worrying to motivate the response? A certain amount of anxiety, or at least some incentive to avoid unpleasant outcomes, is probably a good thing to have, in as much as it helps to ensure that we catch trains on time and so on. But if we found that, on the whole, carrying an umbrella was a good thing because we were likely to be more comfortable with it than without it, this might be an adequate background for learning to carry an umbrella, without specific anxieties being involved. Herrnstein (1969) has pointed out that it is at least theoretically possible for avoidance responses to be learned on the basis of their useful consequences, without any preparatory anxiety, and has designed some ingenious experiments in which rats are prevented from learning when to be anxious, but yet still make avoidance responses.

The basis for the 'avoidance without fear' argument of Herrnstein is avoidance training where there is no warning signal to announce the aversive stimulus. The standard laboratory technique of this kind is the free-operant avoidance procedure introduced by Sidman (1953). In the Skinner box apparatus, very brief shocks are delivered at standard intervals, for instance once every ten seconds. The avoidance response, in this case pressing down the lever, delays the next shock for a period, for instance of eight seconds. The shock can be repeatedly delayed, and the subject therefore has the opportunity of postponing shock indefinitely if it presses the lever at least once every eight seconds. If there is no response, shocks continue at intervals. This procedure has been widely-used to assess avoidance learning abilities in physiological work, and can be effective with a range of time values. The shock-shock interval can be exactly the same as the response-shock interval, or can differ in either direction. The two-factor theory explains this in terms of cycles of anxiety, building up as time passes, being reduced by the responses of lever pressing. Herrnstein, however, suggests that the outstanding characteristic of the free-operant avoidance procedure is simply that subjects are better off if they make avoidance responses than if they don't, and this in itself may be a reasonable cause of the behaviour. Perhaps mild negative reinforcers can support routine behaviours without conditioned waves of fear even though stronger stimuli could result in anxiety or stress.

The distracting effects of anxiety

One way of measuring the force of anxiety is to look for the disruption of customary behaviours. A standard method of doing this is called the conditional emotional response (CER) procedure. A reliable baseline of behaviour is developed and this is used as the background for assessing the distracting effects of a warning signal. Laboratory animals are kept busy responding on a variable interval schedule for food reinforcement (p. 83). At irregular intervals a signal (a buzzer, say) comes on for about a minute, and is at first ignored. This is evident from the fact that the animal carries on its operant task, perhaps finding and eating food while the signal is present. But if the warning signal is used as a precursor for an electric shock, it quickly becomes a disruptive stimulus; the animal may cease its normal work altogether for the duration of the signal, even though this means missing possible food deliveries. Clearly, although working at the food reinforced task is not punished – the animal may go on working without making things worse – anticipation of the aversive stimulus has suppressed the ongoing behaviour. The incipient shock 'puts off' the subject, and this *conditioned suppression* may still happen after prolonged experience of the schedule. The off-putting effect is a very good index of the association between the signal and the aversive stimulus.

Punishment

In view of the desire of everybody to escape from unpleasant situations and associated signals, there have always been reservations and misgivings about inflicting pain or distress on other people, or indeed other animals, as a means of education or reform. Decline in culturally-sanctioned use of corporal punishment can be taken as a dimension of social advance. However fines, imprisonment, threat, insult and rejection are still an intrinsic part of legality and, to a lesser extent, education. The liberal attitude is that using punishment to suppress socially undesirable behaviours is immoral, and also produces undesirable side-effects of stress and aggression. Skinner (1953) and many others have hoped that positive reinforcement, and other means of encouraging good behaviours, could replace the social use of punishment altogether.

For the purposes of experiment punishment can be defined as the reduction of certain behaviour by means of contingent events. Punishment can be looked at as the dark side of positive reinforcement: if responses bring about good stimuli they flourish, but responses that bring about bad stimuli dwindle away. This was the version of mechanical hedonism expressed by Thorndike's original Law of Effect (Ch. 1), in which gain or gratification stamped in causal behaviours while annoyance or loss stamped them out again. Theoretical confusion was introduced by the failure of some weak punishments used by Thorndike and Skinner to produce much dwindling away of persistent behaviours. In Thorndike's case he found that saying 'wrong' after students had given a mistranslation did little to prevent them making further mistakes. Skinner was overimpressed by the short-lived nature of response suppression which resulted from slap-back movements of the bar in his conditioning apparatus. It is now perfectly clear that the discouragement of actions by contingent punishment is if anything a stronger influence on behaviour than the incentive effects of positive reinforcers, as far as laboratory work with animals is concerned (Cambell and Church, 1969). The problem with punishment is not that it always is ineffective, but that it has the unpleasant side-effects of stress, anxiety, withdrawal and aggression in the subject.

The basic suppressive effect of punishing stimuli is illustrated in Figure 5.1. Rats with previous experience of pressing a lever on a fixed interval schedule of reinforcement were given electric shocks every time they pressed the lever, for a fifteen-minute period only. Then they were left to respond freely, being given neither food nor shocks. Different groups of these rats had been given different levels of shocks and the rate of response following punishment depended on the voltage. A low voltage shock did not slow down responding appreciably when it was delivered, but reduced the total number of responses given in the next nine daily hours of extinction testing. A high voltage shock stopped response in most of the subjects almost entirely while it was being delivered and for the remaining nine days of the experiment.

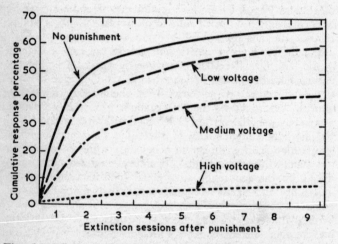

Fig. 5.1 *Effect of punishment on extinction.* (After Boe and Church, 1967: see text for explanation)

This indicates a return to the original conception of reward and punishment as response consequences which have opposite effects on behaviour. Reinforcement strengthens and encourages while punishment on the whole weakens and discourages. Specialized mechanisms and side-effects apply unequally to the reinforcers and punishers, but in many circumstances actions represent a balance between attraction and reluctance built up by favourable and unfavourable outcomes (Mackintosh, 1974). Few responses have universally good consequences, and compensations may be found in apparently unrelieved gloom. Not many behaviours are therefore without some degree of what Miller (1944) called *approach-avoidance conflict*. Animals drawn towards a goal by food may also be repelled by previous punishments received at the goal, and in such cases may be seen to approach and then withdraw from the goal alternately. Given a choice between two goals, each of which represents a mixture of good and bad consequences, it is reasonable to choose the best mixture. The effects of various mixtures of food reward and electric shocks on choices made by rats has been studied by Logan (1969). The animals had equal lengths of experience with certain rewards and punishments given for running down white or black alleys before having the opportunity of choosing between the two alternative alleys. If given seven pellets of food for the white choice against one pellet for the black, they had a strong preference for the larger amount of food, which was only partly outweighed even by a strong shock. An initially strong preference was also evident for the immediate receipt of three pellets as opposed to an identical amount of food delayed for twelve seconds; however, this preference was more readily counteracted by having to run across the electrified grid before reaching the food, and was reversed when the punishment was at a high intensity. Logan interprets this result to mean that some effects of punishment are symmetrically opposite to those of reward, punishment being said to supply *negative incentive* which can cancel out the positive incentive due to reinforcement.

From this point of view, neither the effects of punishment, nor those of reinforcement, can be judged without reference to the other. This fits in with many other results. For instance, the conditioned suppression effects mentioned in the last section depend very much on the degree of positive incentive: suppression is greatest when it does not seriously interfere with the gaining of positive reinforcers.

Furthermore, the effects of punishment are much more pronounced if they are combined with reinforcement, instead of being in opposition to it. One way to do this is to punish response A, at the same time giving plenty of positive reinforcement for response B, where making response B makes it impossible to perform response A as well (Azrin and Holtz, 1966).

Natural defensive reactions to aversive stimuli

A great focus of attention in recent years has been the degree to which *species-specific* behaviours change the effects of learning and reinforcement. 'Species-specific' is a noncommital way of discussing factors which might be instinctive or innate. Analysis of naturally-occurring behaviour patterns has made great strides under the influence of ethologists such as Lorenz and Tinbergen (see D2) and there is a need to integrate ethological results with laboratory findings (Hinde, 1970). It has long been thought that the natural reactions of animals to aversive stimuli, such as running away, panic or 'freezing' in a rigid posture, could facilitate or interfere with learning processes, and these effects are now being studied in more detail (Bolles, 1970). Where it is possible to get away from a source of unpleasantness, most animals have an in-built tendency to do so, by running, leaping, flying or any other method at their disposal. It is suggested that the presence of aversive stimuli, whether as negative reinforcers in escape and avoidance learning, or as punishers, will predispose the animal to these natural reactions. If the subject is required to perform a response which is *compatible* with its first impulses, learning will be facilitated, but if a learning task involves responses which are *incompatible* with natural reactions, the task will be extremely difficult. An extreme case of this occurs with the much-studied button-pecking response of pigeons. Although pecking is maintained under almost all conditions where food has been present in the immediate environment, and there is an identifiable visual cue, it is virtually impossible to persuade a pigeon to peck a key to avoid an electric shock (Herrnstein and Loveland, 1972). It can be done, but only with shocks of critical intensity, which motivate the response without inducing competing behaviours. Running or jumping to get away from the location of shocks is on the other hand a very easily-learned response. Although it is quickly learned, it may be difficult to alter by punishment once it has been established. Rats trained to run away from shock in a start box down an electrified alley to a 'safe' box will continue to run over the electrified grid, even if the starting box is made 'safe', and even if the response has once been allowed to die out when the entire maze has been made 'safe'. Dogs trained to jump over a hurdle to *escape* shocks may be unable to alter this pattern when they are jumping from a safe compartment over to a live one. Natural responses, once learned, are very persistent.

72

Apart from merely running away, hiding or returning to familiar quarters are common responses to dangerous or aversive situations, but have rarely been investigated. A third alternative is the 'freezing' response. This is often part of the response pattern in the confined space of the operant-conditioning chamber, and sometimes contributes to the conditioned suppression effect.

Stimulus compatibility. The conditioning of emotional reactions to new stimuli is usually studied with rather artificial cues such as buzzers and flashing lights being associated with electric shocks. There are some more natural combinations which allow conditioning to occur more rapidly. For rats, tastes go with sickness so that an animal given an emetic drug will tend to lose interest in the last food tasted before intestinal upset began, even if the last meal was quite some time before the illness (up to several hours). On the other hand, tastes do not go with external factors, and so the external unpleasantness of electric shocks is connected with the place where it happened, rather than with what was being eaten at the time. It is not clear whether this effect is due to previous experience that internal signals go with internal consequences while external signals go with external events, or whether there is some 'wired-in' preference for certain kinds of association. There certainly seem to be strong natural aversions to such things as spiders and snakes; and it has been pointed out that many more people have phobias for such objects as these than have phobias for things like furry white lambs. We should not forget, though, that even painful shocks can become attractive if they are associated often enough with positive reinforcers and pleasant stimuli can become aversive after being paired with fear: initial preferences can often be overcome by learning (Pavlov, 1927).

Fighting back

The best form of defence may be attack, especially if it is too late to retreat. It is well known that animals can be most dangerous when they are frightened or cornered, and that people are often more violent when they are depressed, and more irritable when they are anxious. Aggression and fear are entwined physiologically as the 'fight or flight' mode of the autonomic nervous system and in the central control of emotion by the brain (A2). It is not surprising that first reactions to disappointment or fear may be irrational aggression or hate, whether in the case of hostility towards innocent persons after dangerous incidents in motor cars or in the ancient practice of killing the messenger who brought bad news.

The simplest stimulus for aggression may be pain. Animals will substitute attack for escape if another animal is present when shocks are given. Even inappropriate objects like stuffed dolls and rubber balls may elicit threat postures or be scratched and bitten if the floor of an animal's cage is suddenly electrified. After being shocked, a pigeon or rat will move across the cage to attack another animal, and monkeys have been trained to press levers so that a ball is presented for them to bite. Being shocked, therefore, can be said to induce a mood of aggression, and in that mood animals do go to some trouble to engage in attack (Hinde, 1970).

Other aversive situations may also induce aggression. One of the first behavioural categories discussed by Pavlov is the 'freedom reflex' by which he meant the struggling and fighting which frequently accompanied the first attempts to restrain the movements of a dog by a harness. Some process of taming is needed before most animals will put up with physical confinement or handling without showing aggression. Loss of freedom of movement because of physical restraint may be paralleled as a source of resentment and aggression by intensive social restraints in human institutions.

Being told what to do, or being prevented from doing things by bureaucratic restrictions or cultural taboos, can perhaps be classified as a form of *frustration*. Frustration has sometimes been defined as the prevention of a highly-motivated response, though more recently it has been interpreted as the absence or loss of rewards (Amsel, 1972). We regard it as self-evident that if trains are repeatedly cancelled, it is more likely that normally impassive bowler-hatted commuters will show violence towards railway staff, even if the personnel at hand have no responsibility for the cancellations. Somehow the inconvenience and aversiveness of waiting, or the loss of the routine reinforcers of catching a train after getting to the station, brings about aggression, whether or not it is 'justified'. Such aggression does not always take the form of violence. Vocal abuse and postural threats are frequent preliminaries to, or substitutes for fighting in human and animal confrontations and even more diverse expressions of aggression are possible. In one experiment designed to induce frustration heavy smokers were kept up all night, not being allowed to sleep, smoke, read or otherwise amuse themselves. They were led to expect an early morning meal which was cancelled at the last moment. As predicted, this produced decidedly uncomplimentary comments directed at the psychologists running the experiment. Further aggression was shown in later paper and pencil tests when a subject produced grotesque drawings of dismembered and disembowelled human bodies, said to represent 'psychologists'. The expressions of hostility engendered by disappointment and frustration are more limited in laboratory animals, but the emotional effects of not getting the usual food reinforcer can be strong enough to induce prolonged attacks on another animal of the same species (e.g. Azrin *et al.*, 1966).

It is extremely important to consider the influence of aversive stimuli on aggression as one of the adverse effects of negative reinforcers. But reaction to aversive conditions is only *one* of the many factors which influence aggression. Competition and aggression are closely interlocked with social dominance, sexual behaviour and defence of home territories in many animal species (Lorenz, 1966). For us, social and cultural conditioning, especially by imitation learning (Ch. 9) is the overriding monitor of individual aggressiveness (Bandura, 1973).

Aversive stimuli may damage your health

It is possible to worry a good deal without getting ulcers, but worry and anxiety, or more generally *stress*, may be responsible not only for ulcers but also for proneness to heart attacks, lowered resistance to diseases and other health risks, besides endangering mental stability. Some of the conditions which cause this kind of stress may be very complicated, but there is little doubt that intense aversive stimuli can contribute to it. Recent theories and experiments have concentrated on the subsidiary psychological circumstances that might make a certain amount of physical pain more or less 'stressful'. The degree of stress is gauged by bodily changes such as loss of weight or ulceration of the stomach, and psychological changes such as inability to learn new problems. Generally, it appears that uncertainty and conflict compound the stressful effects of receiving electric shocks, but the degree of stress is considerably relieved by the experience of being able to 'cope' with the aversive stimuli by successful escape or avoidance responses (Weiss, 1971).

Other factors such as prolonged confinement and lack of rest may also exacerbate stress. The best-known example is the 'executive monkey' experiment (Brady, 1958). Monkeys were paired together on a free-operant avoidance schedule, so that only one monkey, the 'executive', could make avoidance responses, but both monkeys received the same shocks. In fact, the executive monkeys worked so hard, making hundreds of responses per hour, that shocks were very infrequent, only about one per hour. The shift-work system was unusually demanding: six hours on then six hours off, all day every day. A few weeks of this produced sever ulceration of the stomach for the 'executives' but not for the other monkeys. However, with less rigorous work schedules, being the 'executive' may often seem less stressful; it is usually less upsetting to be the driver than the passenger in a badly-driven fast car. Certainly it seems in experiments with rats, that ability to take evasive action moderates stress. With a different schedule from the 'executive monkeys', 'executive rats', whose actions determined the shocks received by them and a second animal, had more normal weight gains and far fewer ulcers than their passive partners. In these cases the 'executives' did not work excessively, and the passive animals received quite a few shocks. The unpredictability of shocks may increase stress for the passive animal, while achievement of some 'safe' periods reduces stress for the executive.

The unpredictability of unpleasant events may not only produce more stress, but may diminish future capacity to deal with more orderly and avoidable aversive stimuli. It has been proposed that exposure to random shocks, which an animal can do nothing to escape or avoid, leads to a state of *learned helplessness* which prevents further efforts to learn in related situations (Maier *et al.*, 1969). There certainly seem to be cases of 'giving up' in experiments where dogs are given inescapable shocks before training in a shuttle-box task. Although this task is usually learned very rapidly (p. 65), complete failure to learn can be found in dogs with previous experience of enforced failure.

Thus, although the picture is far from clear, the intensive use of negative reinforcers and punishing stimuli can be accompanied by risks to physical and emotional health, especially if combined with uncertainty and conflict.

Therapeutic use of aversive stimuli

It may seem odd, in view of the damaging effects of aversive stimuli discussed in the last two sections, that unpleasant stimuli could ever be employed therapeutically (see F3). There are two reasons why therapeutic uses for negative reinforcement and punishment can be found. First, there may be problems such as alcoholism or self-injury which it is felt are serious enough to outweigh the disadvantages of aversive stimulation. Second, not all unpleasant experiences are harmful, and a certain amount of stress may even be found invigorating or interesting, without leading to emotional disaster. A modicum of stress in early life may actually be a prerequisite to later psychological adjustment. In any event, mild negative reinforcers need not always be damaging, and can sometimes be used to bring long-term benefits.

Time-outs to reduce problem behaviours. A standard form of mild punishment which has been used to deal with several kinds of disruptive behaviour in children is termed a *time-out*. The essential part of this is to remove the child from any possible social reinforcement for problem behaviours such as temper tantrums. Usually the time-out consists of five or ten minutes of social isolation. As a consistent consequence of the offending behaviour, the child is placed alone in his bedroom, or possibly in a room reserved for time-out purposes, and stays there for the minimum period, or for longer if the problem behaviour continues. It has been reported that this technique diminishes otherwise intractable behaviour problems, with no undesirable side-effects. An early case was that of Dicky, who after having had serious eye operations when he was two years old was hospitalized as a childhood schizophrenic when only three (Wolf *et al.*, 1964). A critical problem was that he needed to wear spectacles to safeguard his sight, but did not do so. He was shaped up to wear glasses with food reinforcers (Ch. 3) but developed a habit of taking them off and throwing them across the room about twice a day. To suppress this behaviour, Dicky was simply put in his room for ten minutes if he threw his glasses, and not allowed out if he threw a tantrum. He stopped throwing his glasses after five days. The same time-out procedure was also used initially to reduce the frequency of Dicky's tantrums, which included self-destructive behaviours such as head-banging and face-scratching.

Time-outs in the form of removal from the dining room were used to eliminate food-throwing and food-stealing. After these and some other training methods for improving bedtime behaviour and socially appropriate speech, performed with the cooperation of the parents, Dicky was able to return home and showed continued progress six months later.

Time-outs may not be very strong aversive stimuli; their effect may be due to loss of positive reinforcers. But there is no hard and fast distinction between situations which are aversive because they signify loss of social rewards and situations that are lonely or unpleasant in themselves. It has been found, though, that social isolation procedures can be very much more effective than the use of differential attention by parents. Wahler (1969) described the treatment of children whose parents had sought psychological help because the children were 'oppositional'. That meant they were unresponsive to parental requests or demands and would have tantrums, refuse to go to bed, jump on furniture and so on. Even when the parents were successfully trained to ignore 'bad' behaviours completely but reinforce 'good' behaviours immediately by giving attention and approval, the behaviour of the children did not improve. The parents were then instructed and supervised in the use of the time-out technique of isolating children in their bedrooms immediately after oppositional behaviours, but giving approval for cooperative activities. This produced dramatic and sustained changes in the children's behaviour.

More severe treatments. Traditional methods of 'making the punishment fit the crime' have recently been included in a complex package of techniques applied to persistent behavioural problems such as self-stimulation in autistic children and bed-wetting as well as daytime incontinence in retarded or normal children. Abundant positive reinforcement by social encouragement and food rewards for desirable substitute activities accompany adverse consequences for target behaviours. For instance, programmes for the successful retraining of incontinent adults or children have included some self-correction of accidents – the subject has to wash his own clothes or make his own bed (Azrin *et al.*, 1974).

The most controversial application of punishment and negative reinforcement procedures is the adoption of electric shocks as a stimulus for the training of retarded or autistic children. These are cases where severe treatments are brought into play because there are even more severe behavioural difficulties. If children have to be kept in strait-jackets because they are likely to break their bones or cause dangerous wounds by self-injuring responses, the use of electric shocks to punish self-injury may arguably be less cruel than it might first be thought (Lovaas and Simmons, 1969). It has also been found that autistic children who are completely withdrawn and have virtually no social behaviours can be shaped to some basic social actions such as hugging by the negative reinforcement of escape from electric shocks (Lovaas *et al.*, 1965).

Electrical stimulation and drug-induced nausea have both been used to induce conditioned emotional reactions during aversion therapy (Ch. 2).

Summary and conclusions

Operant conditioning can take the form of learning to get away from frightening or dangerous situations as well as getting closer to positive reinforcers. An act learned or strengthened because it removes or prevents disagreeable sensations is said to be negatively reinforced. A response suppressed or weakened when it is followed by pain or loss of reward is said to be punished. It is necessary to take into account conditioned emotional reactions to stimuli associated with aversive events, since these may influence responses not directly reinforced or punished. Other reactions, such as running away from dangerous situations, or acting aggressively towards other individuals present, may also result. Strong aversive stimuli which are unpredictable, or cause conflict, contribute to stress. Despite these many side effects, negative reinforcement and punishment have occasional therapeutic applications.

6
Intermittent reinforcement and extinction: scarcity and absence of reinforcers

'If at first you don't succeed, try, try and try again.' It is often necessary to make several attempts before achieving a goal. However generously we define a response, it is always possible to find responses which have to be repeated without result. Several rabbits might have to be chased for each one that is caught, several shots might be needed to get a golf ball in the hole, several shops may need to be searched before we find the pair of shoes we like. Searching and looking are the most obvious kind of behaviour where persistence is intermittently rewarded, but the extreme example of gambling, where rewards may be not only rare, but apparently inadequate, suggests that very persistent behaviour may be maintained by rewards that are extremely infrequent. Subsidiary or compensatory rewards may help fill the gap. Dogs obviously enjoy chasing rabbits even if they don't catch them (see Ch. 7), individual golf shots are rewarded by getting closer to the hole and so on. Many goals occur so infrequently that goal-directed behaviour has to be reinforced by the achievement of sub-goals, and ancillary benefits. If, for instance, you decide to sail around the world single-handed, then the preparations have to be either enjoyable in themselves, or pursued because they bring the final goal nearer. Many of the sub-goals and subsidiary rewards can be discussed as *secondary reinforcers* or parts of *response chains* that are systematically related to major or *primary* reinforcers involved (Ch. 7).

However, the most dramatic discovery of research in operant

conditioning is that the behavioural effects of individual reinforcers can grow with extended training so that the same reinforcer which originally generated one response comes to command literally thousands of responses of the same kind. A chimpanzee which starts by hesitantly pushing a button once for each food reward may after long training get through 4,000 pushes for each reward. But what is the limit to this process? Does it mean that four hundred thousand, or four million responses can be learned just as easily, or that eventually the rewards won't matter at all? That can't be true, because lack of reinforcement must eventually bring about the *extinction* or the disappearance of the reinforced response, according to all the textbooks. There is obviously a paradox here, if lack of reinforcers can sometimes produce thousands of responses, and at other times produce the dwindling away of the response called extinction. In fact in the laboratory we can tell fairly well when cutting out reinforcers will extend the range of responses and when it will cause extinction. However this still leaves us with another unexpected result, because extinction is slower after sparse and infrequent reinforcement than after rich and continuous reinforcement. This is called the *partial reinforcement effect*, which is one of the easiest phenomena to reproduce, but one of the most difficult to explain.

Apart from the partial reinforcement effect of greater response persistence found with less reinforcement, the interest in intermittent reinforcement schedules lies in different patterns of behaviour produced by different schedules of intermittent reinforcement. These schedules were briefly described in Chapter 3.

Intermittent schedules of reinforcement

A convenient visual display representing performance on simple schedules of reinforcement can be obtained with a *cumulative recorder*. More elaborate recordings of exact times when various responses are made can be achieved by storing data on magnetic tape for later computer analysis, but cumulative records give a useful general impression of the patterns of responding. When the records are presented as in Figure 6.1 it is important to remember that a horizontal line means that nothing is happening, whatever the level of the line. Horizontal distance measures time, and vertical distance gives the total number of responses made. The *slope* of the record corresponds to the *rate of response*, which is a valuable measure on basic schedules of reinforcement. In Figure 6.1 records for each of the four basic reinforcement schedules have been put together for comparison. Typical schedule performance, and extinction curves for each schedule, are shown. The performance curves represent samples of behaviour after considerable experience of the schedule. It usually takes many hours for animals to learn a particular schedule under conventional laboratory conditions, but after that behaviour should not vary much from day to day if health and weight of the animal, and environmental factors such as temperature, remain constant.

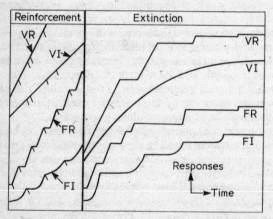

Fig. 6.1 *Cumulative records of reinforced responding and extinction with basic schedules of reinforcement* (After Reynolds, 1968)

Many species of animal, including man, have been tested on the schedules of reinforcement mentioned in Figure 6.1. When an appropriate combination of response and reinforcer is selected (see Ch. 7) the basic patterns of response, and the differences between the schedules, can be observed in all species tested. The standard training procedure is to allow for experience of continuous reinforcement of a response before intermittent reinforcement is introduced. Training on interval schedules of reinforcement is much easier than training for ratio schedules because low response rates in the early stages of training do not prevent the subject from receiving reinforcement.

Fixed interval schedules. Eventual performance when fixed time intervals separate reinforcements (Fig. 6.1) shows the highest rates of response just before reinforcement becomes due. On average, rate of response increases as time passes since the last reinforcement, and this often can be seen on individual cumulative records. It has been shown that the passage of time, rather than chaining of responses, is the important stimulus.

Fixed ratio schedules. Care is necessary for training on fixed ratio schedules. A rat previously reinforced for every lever press would never learn to respond successfully if put immediately on to FR 100; it would probably give up responding before 100 responses had been made. A form of gradual shaping can be used by gradually increasing the size of the fixed ratio in steps within the capacity of the subject. Or a fixed ratio may be used after training on an interval schedule. The final performance on fixed ratio schedules has pronounced pauses after each reinforcement. Following the pause the animal reels off the required fixed number of responses very quickly. As with fixed interval schedules there is evidence of anticipation of reward at the appropriate time when the schedule has been learned: detailed measurement has shown that the speed and force of responses increase towards the end of the run.

Variable interval schedules. If reinforcements are obtainable at unpredictable times, rate of response is much steadier than for fixed schedules (Fig. 6.1). However there is still an underlying tendency for response rate to speed up as time passes since the last reinforcement. This is related to the increasing probability of the animal's getting a reinforcement the longer it has been without one. The average rate of response depends on the average interval between reinforcements. If the average intervals are long so that reinforcements are given infrequently, rate of response is lower than if the average interval is short.

Variable ratio schedules. In these schedules an unpredictable number of responses is needed for each reinforcement. As with all ratio schedules, the sooner the subject makes the responses the sooner he gets the reinforcement. Variable ratio schedules can therefore produce high rates of response without pausing after reinforcement, if very long ratios are not introduced too suddenly (Fig. 6.1).

Multiple schedules. Two or more schedules can be learned by the same subject when a distinctive cue is used to signal which schedule is in effect. The chimpanzees shot into space in the early stages of the NASA space programme had to perform several tasks on a multiple schedule. While orbiting the earth they had, among other things, to work on a fixed ratio for food while a yellow light was on, make a separate response for water on a low rate schedule if a green light was on, and make fast shock avoidance responses on the water lever if a red light was on. Multiple schedules reflect real-life situations in that different schedules operate in different situations.

Chain schedules. Responses can be chained together by a method like a multiple schedule, in which each response is performed in a particular stimulus situation. The only difference is that a complete chain of response has to be completed for each reinforcement. A very simple chain would be a schedule for a pigeon to peck ten times on a left-hand button to turn on the light behind the right hand button, and then peck the right-hand button on a variable ratio schedule to produce food.

Concurrent schedules. If more than one schedule is operating at the same time, the subject has to make a continuous series of choices about which response to make next. For instance, a rat could be given a fixed interval schedule on the right-hand lever for food, and a fixed ratio schedule on the left-hand lever for water. In this kind of situation the two responses interfere with each other and neither response would be performed in the normal manner.

Comparison of operant with classical conditioning
The ease of establishing intermittent schedules of reinforcement in operant conditioning is in marked contrast to the weakening effects of intermittent reinforcement in Pavlovian procedures. If a stimulus sometimes signals food and sometimes doesn't, this simply means that it is an unreliable signal as far as classical conditioning goes. But if a *response* sometimes produces food but sometimes doesn't it means that making more responses is

a necessary strategy for obtaining food. With operant schedules of reinforcement, the activity of making numerous responses is rewarded. Although there are several opinions about the interpretation which should be given to disparities between operant and classical conditioning, it is agreed that intermittent reinforcement is an area of dispute. The distinction is between an almost passive absorbing of information in pure classical conditioning and the active organization of behaviour necessary in operant conditioning. This difference between learning *about* reinforcers and learning what to *do* to get reinforcers is amplified when reinforcers are relatively rare events.

Extinction after continuous and intermittent reinforcement
Why does a response die away when reinforcement ceases? The answer seems almost unnecessary – the response was there only because of the reinforcement and when the reinforcement goes, so must the response. It is the supplementary questions which are difficult. Why do responses appear to continue indefinitely after some forms of negative reinforcement (p. 66) or after reinforcement by administration of narcotics to addicted animals? Why does the pattern of responding in extinction reflect the previous schedule of reinforcement? Why are meagrely-rewarded difficult tasks more persistently performed in extinction than easy tasks which have been richly rewarded?

The number of conflicting interpretations given for curious results in extinction procedures is greater than for other areas of learning but there are two distinct themes of explanation. On the one hand extinction performance may reflect emotional upheavals caused by the absence of rewards, and on the other it may reflect cognitive problems to do with 'finding-out' that rewards are no longer available.

Cognitive effects in extinction. The importance of 'finding-out' in extinction of the standard tasks of maze-running and bar-pressing has been demonstrated by 'latent' extinction which occurs when animals are given experience of empty goal boxes or empty food magazines. This experience immediately reduces the vigour of responses previously rewarded from the now empty goal boxes or food magazines. Circumstances which help the subject 'notice the difference' in extinction, such as novel cues or a change in the apparatus, will speed up extinction, while difficulties in finding out about absence of reinforcement prolong extinction. The problems of extinguishing avoidance responses which take the subject out of a situation and thus prevent contact with new information have been mentioned already (p. 66). The perplexities of distinguishing between scarcity and absence of reinforcers must contribute to the continuance of responding after variable schedules of reinforcement (Fig. 6.1). Subjects experienced on a variable ratio schedule of reinforcement shifted to extinction are in the position of someone putting money into a fruit machine which has previously paid off about once every hundred goes, but has surreptitiously been fixed so that it doesn't pay off at all. Even allowing for perfect memory and ideal processing of new information, it would take some time to conclude that the machine had in fact been altered. It is not surprising that if long sequences of non-rewarded responses have eventually been followed by reward, it is more likely that long sequences of non-rewarded responses will be performed in extinction.

Emotional effects in extinction. Perhaps the persistence of responding after negative reinforcement or reinforcement by narcotics is due partly to the emotional intensity of the original learning. Not much work has been done on that problem, but there has been plenty of speculation about the influence of frustration and disappointment when reinforcements are discontinued. Monkeys, as well as children, may have tantrums if an accustomed reward is tampered with – there is little doubt that discontinuing rewards can produce emotional disturbance. Amsel (1972) has investigated frustration in rats running through simple mazes with two goal boxes in which rats run down an alley to get food in the first box, then run from the first to the second box to get more food. If food is left out of the first box, they reveal their frustration by running faster to the second box. Amsel's theory is that the same frustration normally suppresses responding in extinction. Animals who have experienced intermittent reinforcement will have learned to tolerate such frustration, and will therefore go on responding for long periods during extinction. This effect can be seen after intermittent or partial reinforcement has been given for running mazes as well as with variable schedules of reinforcement. If Amsel is right, intermittent reinforcement teaches not only particular response strategies but also more general emotional reactions, so that an animal may learn to 'keep trying' and this will increase the persistence of responses in extinction (see p. 59). The existence of such general response classes might help to explain otherwise puzzling results where animals show more persistence after being trained on arduous tasks such as running up steep inclines.

It may be that experience of conditions where rewards are few and far between leads to persistence in extinction for both cognitive and emotional reasons. The absence of reward is less noticeable after scarcity, response sequences and strategies formed by schedules of reinforcement are not easily disturbed, and emotional resistance to the absence of reward may grow up as a by-product of intermittency of reinforcement.

Intermittent reinforcement and extinction in human behaviour
The idea of intermittent reinforcement is used more as an explanatory device than as a practical tool in applications of reinforcement theory to human behaviour. It is said that persistent behaviours which have very few apparent rewards may be sustained by occasional reinforcement. Examples are participation in games of chance and in superstitious rituals, where profit may be infrequent or accidental (Skinner, 1953). It may prove feasible to utilize similar schedules of reinforcement in therapy to increase the resistance to extinction of adaptive behaviours.

Extinction itself has sometimes been found effective in the management of behaviour problems in children. If parents consistently ignore behaviour such as bedtime tantrums, it may gradually disappear. In some cases, even severe or self-destructive deviant behaviour will stop when it no longer attracts the attention of onlookers (Lovaas and Simmons, 1969). However Ferster (1961) has pointed out the theoretical dangers of insufficient reaction by parents to the activities of their children. If parents remain impassive in the face of the ordinary range of annoying behaviours it may come about that only bizarre behaviours by the child gain parental attention. It is therefore hazardous for parents to ignore mild misbehaviours if at the same time more extreme acts provoke rewarding social exchanges. Nevertheless the extinction of deviant behaviours has sometimes been accomplished when parents carefully ignore all such responses (Wahler, 1969).

Summary and conclusions

The effects of operant reinforcement can be stretched out so that long periods of activity are devoted to each reinforcer. Standard routines for doing this, schedules of reinforcement, space out rewards in time or according to amounts of response. Although a little reinforcement can be made to go a long way by these means, no reinforcement at all usually causes a gradual withering away of the response pattern previously built up under its influence. For one reason or another, this extinction of behaviours when reinforcement is removed is less immediate after experience of sparse or variable rewards.

7
Primary and secondary reinforcers: where do they come from?

'Feels great' – Like it OK' – 'Happy button' – 'Feel sick all over': these are one patient's subjective descriptions of what it is like to have reinforcement centres aroused through silver wires stuck deep into the brain. Some patients have had as many as fifty leads permanently inplanted in their head, so that very small electrical currents could be delivered to different parts of their brain. The reinforcing effects of the various electrodes are assessed by allowing the individual to press buttons which turn on brief jolts of stimulation (Heath, 1963). Investigations like this are rare, but the findings complement thousands of experiments with rats and monkeys designed to discover exactly what parts of the brain are important for motivation and reinforcement. For the human patient, pressing the 'Feels great' button was accompanied by some sexual images and by the elimination of anxiety and 'bad' thoughts. Animals receiving rewarding brain stimulation indulge in almost every kind of activity including exploration, eating and sexual responses, depending on the precise area or site stimulated (see A2). Although many of the most important details have yet to be settled, study of the brain mechanisms involved in reinforcement is one way of trying to answer the basic questions of 'what is reinforcement?' and 'why are reinforcers reinforcing?' A physiological answer may eventually assist in the matching together of other kinds of information based on behavioural experiments or subjective impressions.

A second kind of answer to the question 'why are reinforcers reinforcing?' can be made in terms of evolution. Unless Darwin was completely mistaken, all species have had to evolve methods of ensuring that they eat enough food, keep away from dangerous or damaging situations and have proper social relationships with their fellows particularly in the context of reproduction. Hull and Skinner were content to leave it at that, and get on with behavioural analyses of reinforcement, but ethologists like Tinbergen and Lorenz have investigated naturally-occurring patterns of behaviour which indicate that animals have evolved a number of methods of adapting their behaviour to the environment, including the development of 'species-specific' reinforcers (see D2). Morris (1968) among others has speculated about the results of human evolution, which may include unique social and intellectual forms of reward.

A third kind of answer is given by emphasizing the importance of individual experience, especially in human cultures. Many rewarding activities – playing the electric guitar, pretending to be a spaceman – are of such recent origin that brain physiology or the sequence of human evolution have very limited relevance to understanding why that in particular functions as a reinforcer. Traditionally behaviourists have laid a great deal of weight on recently acquired *secondary reinforcers* because of the supposed predominance of these in modern societies.

Physiology of reinforcement

The most frequently selected location of electrodes for positive brain reinforcement is the *medial forebrain bundle* which is a bundle of nerve fibres that runs through an area in the middle of the brain called the lateral hypothalamus (see A2). This gives very strong and reliable reinforcing effects, with animals pressing levers to obtain stimulation almost to exhaustion. It is not at all clear that this is a single 'centre' for positive reinforcement rather than a concentrated pathway for nerve impulses connected with rewarding processes. It is possible to claim, though, that there are separate anatomical locations for positive and negative reinforcement, with the medial forebrain bundle (MFB) the main pathway for reward and the *periventrical system* (PVS) the area for negative reinforcement (Stein, 1969). Stimulation of the PVS has most of the effects that are produced by electrical shocks, and stimulation of the MFB is roughly equivalent to external rewards like food and water. In order to use MFB stimulation in schedules of reinforcement it is necessary to allow rats several self-produced shots for each 'reward'. The technique is to have the rat press twenty times (for instance) at the right-hand lever. As the reward for this a left-hand lever is activated so that the rat can give itself 100 brief pulses of current through wires going down into its brain. Used like this MFB stimulation produces results similar to that of food given to hungry animals (Pliskoff *et al.*, 1965). There is little difficulty in showing that responding can be suppressed by punishment with PVS stimulation.

There are thus reasonable grounds for the hypothesis that the behavioural difference between positive and negative reinforcement is partly produced by separate physiological processes. A more tentative suggestion is that there may be chemically different systems for the incentive and response-shaping functions of positive reinforcement (Crow, 1973). It is known that the transmission of impulses in many neural pathways requires the release of the chemical *noradrenalin*, while certain other pathways make use of a different agent, *dopamine*. Both kinds have been identified in the MFB but it is possible to find places where only one kind operates. Rats pressing a lever for stimulation at 'dopaminergic' sites move forward bright-eyed and eager, sniffing at the lever and actively exploring the surrounding region. In marked contrast, rats self-stimulating at 'noradrenergic' sites press dully and mechanically with little apparent enthusiasm. Whatever the final verdict is, it looks as though neurophysiologists will eventually be able to give us a fairly detailed picture of the separate biochemical and neural processes which underly different kinds of reinforcement effect.

At present there is still no agreement about the relative importance of the several possible aspects of reinforcing events: direct effect of stimulus in-put; subjective pleasure; performance of rewarding actions or release from tensions or drives. The dissociation between subjective report and unconscious motivational effects was of course a major aspect of Freud's theories (see D3) and there can be little doubt that reinforcement can take place without intense pleasure or even knowledge on the part of the subject. A hint of this kind of effect is apparent in the data that goes with the subjective descriptions at the beginning of this chapter. The button producing stimulation that was only described as 'Like it OK' was actually pressed a third as much again as the 'Happy button' and almost as much as the 'Feels great' button. Even more responses were given on a button that produced subjective irritability rather than pleasure! The behavioural reinforcing power of a stimulus cannot accurately be judged from someone's own sensations, although on the whole things which people say they like should work as reinforcers.

The release from tensions or reduction of drives is one way of describing reinforcement by escape from pain or anxiety. However, it has proved to be a very minor part of positive reinforcement with food or brain stimulation (A2, D2). Escape from hunger is less important than positive incentive for food, as far as this can be shown from laboratory experiment. A good deal of knowledge about the way the hypothalamus controls motivation for eating has now accumulated (A2; Nisbett, 1972) but it is all consistent with the simple fact that nutritional re-requirements are rather remote from the short-term reinforcement for eating. It is the stimulus properties of taste and smell, if not the pleasure of eating, which reinforce, as is evidenced by rats' liking for sacharrin and most people's tendency to overeat, given the opportunity.

It is extremely hard to disentangle the various pushes and pulls given by sensation alone or by actions connected with sensation. Responses such as eating and drinking, often referred to as *consummatory* acts, may serve as reinforcers. Indeed one view is that activities are the essential thing about reinforcement, in the sense that 'eating' rather than 'food' is what matters most. A special kind of impulse to respond, which some authors believe is the prototype for all reinforcement, is produced when animals receive electric stimulation of the MFB and hypothalamus (Valenstein *et al.*, 1970). The same kind of stimulation which can be used as a reward actually provokes a range of species-specific or instinctive responses. When several electrodes are implanted in the same animal, an experimenter may 'turn on' different behaviours by directing current to particular points in the brain. Dramatic demonstrations have been given of 'radio-controlled' changes in the charging of fighting bulls. Rats can be made to shift from eating to copulating and back again at the flip of a switch (Caggiula, 1970).

The interesting thing as far as theories of motivation go is that such electrical control is *not* mechanical firing of reflexes, but induction of a mood, or incentive to respond. This is easiest to imagine in the case of sexual responses, where the brain stimulation causes sexual excitement which is a reward in itself, but also creates incentive for further sexual activity. The same kind of thing happens, with activation of different parts of the hypothalamus, for other responses like fighting, eating or drinking. It also seems that sometimes a particular electrode produces an incentive to 'do something' without strict boundaries on the behaviour, so that rats get used to doing whatever is available when they are first stimulated. An example is rats learning to run back and forth inside a large box to turn current to their hypothalamus on and off. They would do this anyway, but if given small objects at the place where the current turned on, they always carry something to the other side. The conclusion to be drawn from this set of results is not obvious, but it seems as though one of the jobs of the reinforcement mechanism in the hypothalamus is to make animals do things in their repertoire of instinctive responses. Intimately connected with this function is the facility for making animals do things which are only indirectly part of their natural repertoire, like pressing levers, and allowing them to learn to behave in these new ways.

Evolution and reinforcement

The discovery that natural patterns of behaviour like attack movements can be elicited by electrical stimulation of the brain, even in animals who have never had the chance to exhibit the behaviour before, has helped to rekindle interest in the 'wired-in' or instinctive influences on learning (see A2), by which each species of animal is 'prepared' or constrained so that some responses are more easily learned than others, or that some reinforcers will only work for naturally appropriate responses (Seligman, 1970, Hinde and Stevenson–Hinde, 1973). Each species may have some idiosyncratic forms of learning or types of response. However, the general importance of defensive reactions and 'running-away' with negative reinforcement has been mentioned in Chapter 5, and approach reactions to food, and orienting and exploration in response to unfamiliar stimuli, also show some degree of uniformity between species. Evolutionary factors are of critical importance in determining what activities and stimuli serve as reinforcers for particular species, and the range of possible behaviours that are amenable to each reinforcer.

Food is used so often in experiments because it is an extremely reliable and powerful reinforcer which will motivate a wide range of responses in most animals. The type of food which is reinforcing may of course be species-specific and certain types of 'food-getting' responses, such as pecking in birds and hunting in carnivores, are pre-learned or 'prepared' to a greater or lesser extent. For other reinforcers appropriate behaviours are also constrained. Migration and reproduction must involve strong reinforcers, but the range of behaviours which occur in the natural habitat of any species is usually very narrow. This does not mean that unnatural types of response cannot be learned; although it is certainly not part of either sex's natural mating pattern, both male and female rats will learn to press levers to gain access to a sexually attractive partner, in much the same way that they press levers to obtain food. Rodents apparently press levers for almost anything that has been tried as a reinforcer, including the opportunity to dig sand or shred up paper for nests. But it is not the case that all reinforcers can reinforce all responses – grooming responses are not reinforced very well by food for instance.

Specialized reinforcement processes may be involved in the development of social attachments during infancy (see C3). A remarkably rapid fixation of social attachment to whatever object is around at the time occurs during the first twenty-four hours of the life of birds like ducks or geese, where it normally ensures that the young birds follow their mother (this is termed *imprinting*). A much slower process of socialization takes place in mammals, but it is often found that the proper operation of social and sexual reinforcers in adult life depends on social experience as an infant. It is a moot point whether either the rapid imprinting process or the slower development of social attachment are 'highly prepared' or instinctive responses, but Hoffman and Ratner (1973) persist with the notion that certain innate forms of reinforcement provide the basis for both phenomena.

As in most instances of the *nature/nurture* controversy, there is no way to separate built-in and acquired influences on motivation because normal development requires that these influences act jointly. However species-specific limitations have been suggested, even for the human species. Some facial signals, such as enlarged pupils, are said to have in-built sexual attractiveness. Desmond Morris suggested that the importance attached to female breasts derived from the primate fascination with buttocks. Rather more credibility can be given to the careful study of facial expression in primates (monkeys and apes) which has

94

implied that smiling and laughing in man evolved as separate emotional responses. The consensus of ethological opinion is that there is a considerable measure of innate influence on human social reinforcers, starting with contact comforts in maternal attachment (Harlow, 1958) and continuing with smiling and being smiled at, expressions of greeting and so on (Hinde, 1972). It is always worth bearing in mind, however, the constant modification and attenuation of any human 'prepared' responses by social and cultural experience. Watching colour television and riding in cars are two powerful modern reinforcers. To an extent we could say that they depend on innate preferences – one has to have the physiological equipment for colour vision, and possibly some preference for bright or colourful objects. Riding in vehicles seems to be reinforcing for chimpanzees, and could thus be described as some innate primate value! But the major determinant of the power of televisions and cars as reinforcers is surely a set of experiences and learned attitudes within a particular culture.

Secondary reinforcers

Because individual experience is bound to attentuate or enhance in-built reinforcers – even the 'innate' behaviours coming from brain stimulation can be changed by training – there can be no hard and fast distinction between those reinforcers determined by evolution and those relatively independent of it. But it is convenient to distinguish roughly between a category where the necessary biological function of reinforcers is fairly obvious – traditionally food, water, pain and sex – and a category where biological function is remote. *Primary reinforcers* are the more directly biological ones, *secondary reinforcers* more arbitrary or artificial.

Another scheme for classifying reinforcers, put forward by Premack (1965), removes the need for a two-way classification. He proposed that all behaviours can be considered in the light of a single scale of *reinforcement value* based on the preferences of an individual subject or of a particular animal species. Premack's hypothesis is that activities at the top of the scale will reinforce behaviours further down, but not vice-versa. Most people would agree that the incentive for working overtime is related to more preferred activities which demand the spending of money. It is less obvious that watching television would reward mowing the lawn, but contingencies like this are often set up for children as in 'you must clean up your room before you go out to play'. However, position on a scale of preference should vary according to deprivation conditions and the factor of habituation (Ch. 1), as well as temporary shifts of circumstance.

Secondary reinforcement through pairing

One way in which stimuli which have no intrinsic biological value can become reinforcers is through pairing with a strong reinforcer. Sights and sounds which are a prelude to reinforcing tastes acquire the capacity to act as reinforcers in standard animal learning tasks. It can be arranged that arbitrary objects or signs become desirable simply because they have been presented in close contiguity with another incentive. The presence of attractive young women in close physical proximity to a motor-car, cigar or aeroplane may enhance the rewarding properties of those items, because of involuntary classical conditioning or something of the sort (see Ch. 2). Long-lasting secondary reinforcement has been demonstrated with children by pairing originally boring stimuli such as geometric shapes or 'nonsense syllables' (like MYV or KEB) with sweets or money. For instance, five- to seven-year-olds were given a game of fishing envelopes out of a 'lucky-dip' apparatus. Some envelopes contained sweets, and others stones, depending on the nonsense syllables written on the outside. Even three weeks after the game, the children showed a large difference between their evaluations of the 'good' and 'bad' nonsense syllables. The context of the verbal evaluation was broadened by writing 'KEB', 'MYV' etc. as identifying labels across the chests of drawings of other children. After the different nonsense syllables had been paired with winning or losing money in a gambling game the subjects were asked 'Would you like to play with KEB?', 'Is MYV a nice boy?' and similar questions. Favourable answers were given when the imaginary playmate had been paired with winning money, and unfavourable answers if the association had been with losing (Parker and Rugel, 1973). Two theoretical issues are linked with the formation of secondary reinforcers (sometimes called *conditioned reinforcers*). First, what information is supplied by the pairing? Second, what is the importance of responses given to the secondary reinforcing stimulus? As with secondary negative reinforcers produced by giving signals for shock (p. 68), a neutral cue is a better signal, and a better secondary reinforcer if it carries plenty of information about the primary reinforcer. If it is unreliable, or unnecessary, as a predictor of the primary reinforcer, it has less secondary reinforcing effect. On the other hand, it seems to enhance secondary reinforcing effects if the secondary stimulus calls for a definite response (that is, if it is a *discriminative stimulus*).

Both these theoretical factors may help to make *tokens* very effective as conditioned reinforcers. A token is usually a tangible object like a coin or marble, which is exchangeable for physical rewards. As they are exchangeable, tokens are a reliable index for the primary reinforcer and the responses to do with collecting or handing them in guarantee their discriminative function. Another advantage of token reinforcers is that they can be swopped for a great variety of other rewards, or *back-up reinforcers*. Money can be viewed as the token reward par excellence but in real life is complicated by economic and social variables like savings and investment. Enclosed arrangements called *token economies* have been in vogue in recent years as a method of large scale 'behavioural engineering' in mental hospitals (F3 and B4). Patients are helped by shaping or instructions to perform tasks within their capabilities for the tokens. Self-care and ward-cleaning work, as well as more demanding jobs such as secretarial or laundry work, are rewarded with tokens. Written credits, points or money can be used as tokens, but in the initial attempts metal disc 'coins' were used which could only be obtained on the ward (Ayllon and Azrin, 1968). Virtues ascribed to tokens include: (a) they can be given immediately after a target response, as a direct reinforcement; (b) they are an unambiguous indication of approval; (c) if sufficient back-up reinforcers are available, there are fewer problems of satiation than with food or social reinforcers.

Organizational problems and difficulties of assessment make it hard to evaluate the general usefulness of the all-inclusive token economy method (Kazdin and Bootzin, 1972). But small scale 'token systems' – where, for instance, children may be given tokens which can be exchanged for a variety of toys or sweets – are a valuable addition to more direct methods of reinforcement. The evils of all-inclusive token economies seem to reflect those traditionally ascribed to money: some persons may be tempted to steal other person's tokens, or lend out tokens at exorbitant rates of interest. Very careful supervision is required.

The complexities of the therapeutic application of token reinforcement are less apparent in the experimental study of tokens as reinforcers for animals. Chimpanzees can be trained to perform on various schedules of reinforcement to obtain poker chips if these may later be used to obtain food from a slot-machine (e.g. Kelleher, 1958), though they work harder to obtain poker chips as the time approaches when the exchange can take place. Similarly, rats have been trained to press a lever to produce marbles which can later be dropped in a hole to release food.

Secondary reinforcement through remote associations.
Objects which can be carried around and exchanged for food or sights and sounds which are necessary precursors to primary reinforcement can hardly *not* be associated with their back-up reinforcers. Some transfer of powers of reinforcement can also be observed when the association between the secondary and primary rewards is less obvious. It has always been assumed by Freudians that many of our civilized activities are motivated not by the apparent reinforcers, but by deeper primary drives which the notional rewards represent (D2). Nail-biting is said to occur as some kind of substitute for a more drastic form of self-mutilation, hoarding of money is enjoyed as an expression of anal retentiveness, and so on. There is no need to go to these lengths, but it is probably necessary to allow for some quite complicated mix-ups of human motives. For example, an original reinforcement by parental approval might enhance the satisfactions of stamp collecting, which might later bear fruit in a dedication to foreign affairs.

There is little of substance to be gained by speculation about individual biographies, for reinforcement theory. On the other hand, an interesting sample of relatively remote secondary reinforcement has come to light as a feature of *second-order* reinforcement schedules. These work in the same way as ordinary schedules (p. 83) except that an alternative stimulus is substituted for the proper reinforcer most of the time. Kelleher (1966) trained pigeons to work on a fixed interval schedule with the most likely reward just a flash of light every two minutes. Every thirtieth flash of light was accompanied by a large food reward. Behaviour was maintained in the usual pattern (see Fig. 6.1) while only light flashes were given as incentives to respond, and the obvious explanation was that light flashes had become conditioned reinforcers through pairing with food. But several other experimenters found that behaviour on similar second-order schedules was sustained even if the food reinforcement took place in the *absence* of the secondary stimulus. Stubbs (1971) concluded that any stimulus change could become a secondary reinforcer so long as it was systematically related to food delivery, even if it was never actually paired with food delivery. This liberates secondary reinforcers from the requirement of happening at the same time as their back-up rewards, and extends the scope of the secondary reinforcement phenomenon.

Reinforcement and motivation

It will not have escaped the reader's notice that I have been using the terminology of reinforcement as a substitute for the goals, purposes, drives or intentions which are more common in everyday speech and in other areas of psychology. The relations between reinforcement and other concepts in motivation is discussed in D2 of this series, and examples of reinforcement in social motives are covered in B1. The advantages claimed for analyses in terms of reinforcement are: (a) they are clearly founded on a bedrock of reference experiments, and (b) it follows that they can easily be translated back to experimental tests or to practical therapeutic measures. The limitations lie in the narrowness of the field to which reinforcement concepts apply with certainty. It remains to be seen exactly how narrow or wide this field will become.

Reinforcement in relation to drives and incentives

Motivational states such as hunger, thirst and sexual desire are sometimes termed *drives*. Drives are accommodated in reinforcement theory in so far as they determine the effectiveness of relevant reinforcers. Deprivation of food makes the animal eat, or perform responses that have previously gained food. Deprivation and other factors which change the strength of reinforced behaviour are said to 'change the effectiveness of the reinforcer'. There are many ways of working up a thirst, but it would be an odd sort of thirst which did not make drinking a more potent reinforcer. Incentives can be closely related to reinforcers if they describe the vigour or enthusiasm, as opposed to skill or accuracy, of reinforced behaviour. Other sources (D2, A2; Cofer and Appley, 1964) deal with relevant theoretical and physiological issues in more depth.

A new research area concerning the effectiveness of reinforcers is the study of *adjunctive behaviours* (Falk, 1972). Animals given small amounts of food at intervals develop startling proclivities for other behaviours such as drinking, or gnawing inappropriate objects. Excessive drinking, termed *schedule-induced polydipsia*, is a powerful enough reinforcer to support fixed ratio schedules of lever-pressing for the 'unnecessary' water. It has also been found that periodic brief shocks sometimes evoke eating, or copulation. The possibility that schedules of one reinforcer may alter the effectiveness of another therefore has to be included as a *setting operation* which changes the energizing or directing influence of the second reinforcer. Such behavioural interactions have to be added to other major factors which can be said *either* to changes drives, *or* to activate and alter the effectiveness of positive and negative reinforcers. Illness, brain injury, drugs and medicines can all produce drastic changes in responsiveness which may conveniently be described as changes in motivation, but more accurately assessed by measurement of reinforced behaviours.

Reinforcement in relation to knowledge and purpose
Are all our purposes reflections of reinforcement contingencies? Skinner maintains that purpose and knowledge could be accounted for by a complete enough list of 'contingencies of reinforcement' (p. 18) but has not produced the list (Skinner, 1974). Most of us are prepared to acknowledge the importance of schedules of reinforcement in the Skinner box, and possibly in children or other people, but wish to draw a line somewhere between conditioning and reasoning where our thoughts and inner purposes take over. In fact it is possible to bring a surprising proportion of psychological facts under the aegis of reinforcement theory, as Skinner has done, but this does not in itself appear to solve many of the traditional puzzles about human knowledge and purpose. Differences between impulse and foresight, conscious and unconscious motives, sensual and intellectual satisfaction and so on are still matters of philosophical as much as scientific argument. It may yet turn out to be helpful to consider all such differences as differences between types of reinforcement. Mischel (1973), however, has pointed

out in the context of theories of human personality, that psychological conceptualization needs ultimately to encompass the three perspectives of operant conditioning, personal variables such as beliefs and values, and subjective experience.

Surely knowledge can be acquired without assistance from reinforcement? We can look out of the window or read a newspaper without either purpose or reinforcement, can we not? This problem has a long history in learning theory, with the consensus being that knowledge may be acquired without reward, but actions need motivating (Ch. 1). Although this distinction is valid if rewards are only external goals, it is still possible to include information as a reinforcer itself, or even to define reinforcement as the modulation of information flow (Atkinson and Wickens, 1971). Even looking out of the window and reading newspapers may depend, if not on tangible profits, on temporary interest, sensory satisfaction or previously gained advantages. The reinforcement theorist may therefore continue to pry his way into areas of psychology where the main inhabitants feel he has no business.

Summary and conclusions
Reinforcement is essentially a behavioural concept, applicable to reliably observed evidence that responses vary according to their effects. The concept is buttressed by physiological research which is uncovering the brain mechanisms responsible for the effects of reinforcement and the subjective pleasures which may or may not accompany it. The evolutionary background to reinforcement is the necessity for arousing and directing instinctive and learned behaviours at appropriate times. Primary reinforcers are those whose biological function is clear, secondary reinforcers those whose powers have been acquired through an association with more powerful rewards or punishments. It is possible to put the question of biological function to one side and rank reinforcers according to the observed preferences of an individual or species.

8
Discrimination learning: reinforcement for paying attention

'Telling the difference' between stimuli is a prerequisite for most other kinds of behaviour. Habituation (see p. 20) allows us in a sense to 'tell the difference' between familiar and unfamiliar stimuli, and it is necessary to take notice of positive or negative reinforcers before any kind of conditioning can begin. In these cases however, we tell the difference without any special effort. Habituation, by definition, does not demand our attention, and an immediate reaction to attractive or aversive stimuli is something that we take for granted. *Discrimination learning* applies to distinctions that we do not make to start with, and might never make but for an adequate programme of training or experience. This description would cover most academic and manual skills, but as the reader may by now expect, the theoretical issues I shall deal with revolve around animal experiments. Discrimination has long been a focus for theoretical analysis, and it is worth looking at some of the behavioural techniques and results divorced from their possible implications in the first instance.

Methods and terms
In both classical and operant conditioning, the occurrence of reinforcement with one stimulus but not with another is likely to have the effect of intensifying responses to the reinforced stimulus and eroding responses to the other one. In either case the reinforced signal may be referred to as the positive stimulus or $S+$, and the non-reinforced cue as the negative stimulus or

$S-$. A positive stimulus of this kind, or a stimulus which has come to act as a sign or cue for a particular response, is said to be a *discriminative stimulus*. In its most obvious form, the discriminative stimulus may call for action in a *GO:NO-GO* or *successive* discrimination. Waiting at traffic lights is a typical GO:NO-GO, with the green light a discriminative stimulus for pulling away, and the red light the $S-$. This example is a good illustration for a frequent characteristic of GO:NO-GO discriminations, which is that waiting around in the NO-GO part is annoying if not actually aversive. To continue with the motoring metaphor, another form of discrimination requires *choice between alternatives*, as in deciding which direction to take at a junction or *choice-point*. For this choice, or *simultaneous discrimination*, there is no waiting period required, although if you don't know the way you might take some time to make up your mind. In laboratory tests of simultaneous discrimination, subjects would be presented with two or more stimuli, and asked to choose the 'correct' one either by naming it or pointing to it, or for animals by touching the correct stimulus or making some similar indicative response. The simultaneous presentation of 'right' and 'wrong' stimuli allows for detailed comparisons of the stimuli to be made and for *relational* effects to be more prominent. Relational discrimination means responding to 'the bigger' or 'the brighter' rather than to a particular size or brightness. In the GO:NO-GO or *successive discrimination* method, only one stimulus is given at a time, and so comparisons are more difficult. It is much easier to detect a forged five-pound note if you have a real one to compare it with.

Another method involving comparisons is the *matching-to-sample* procedure, which is usually given as a choice between two alternatives on either side of a centre sample, but can be much more complicated if for instance children are asked to 'point to a letter like this one'. Pigeons might be given three buttons to look at, and rewarded if they peck whichever button is 'the same as' the middle one. Depending on the number of samples and choices given, there is much more to learn in a matching-to-sample task than in a single 'right or wrong?' discrimination.

Stimulus generalization and stimulus control. Measuring the results of discrimination learning requires finding out if certain stimuli make any difference to behaviour. This is not always as easy as it seems, since a subject who has apparently learned one discrimination may in fact have achieved his success by an alternative method. 'Clever Hans' is a nineteenth-century horse now famous because he was supposed to be able to solve arithmetic problems by tapping out the correct answer, but was found to depend on subtle cues from his trainer. In such cases we say that the question to be answered is 'which stimulus is controlling the behaviour?' Is it the ostensible signal or some other clue to the correct answer? An alternative way of putting the question is to ask 'what stimulus is the subject attending to?' The answer has to be given by carefully isolating the critical feature or features of the environment which are being picked up. In most cases the technique is to alter some aspect of the situation and note any changes in behaviour.

Sometimes it is valuable to make a series of systematic alterations in a discriminative stimulus to judge which feature (or *dimension*) is controlling responses. If a pigeon has learned to peck at a green square and we wish to know whether 'green' or 'position of square' is important, we could present the bird with red, orange, green, yellow and blue squares, in five different positions. We should probably find that the position of

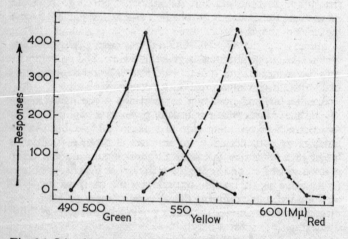

Fig. 8.1 *Stimulus generalization gradients*. These examples could be obtained by reinforcing a pigeon's responses to a particular colour and then showing a number of colours at random, without reinforcement (After Guttman and Kalish, 1956)

the square made no difference, but the curve of number of responses against colour was shaped like figure 8.1, with a dropping off of responses as stimuli become less similar on the dimension of wavelength. Figure 8.1 shows steep *gradients of stimulus generalization*. Provided we are sure the stimuli did not differ in brightness or any other indirect clues, we can say that the steep gradient shows *stimulus control* for wavelength or, more loosely, 'the pigeon was attending to colour'.

Learning with and without inhibition

Inhibition is a theoretical term, and its exact interpretation is not needed here. It is something which is held responsible for suppressing responses to non-reinforced stimuli. In practice it may consist of strengthening opposite or 'antagonistic' responses, which may be seen as a deliberate 'holding back' of the response, or a turning away from the negative stimulus. An extremely visible kind of inhibition is reported by Konorski (1948). A dog was given food after the signal of a metronome, but if the experimenter bent the dog's leg while the metronome ticked, food was withheld. As the dog learned that having a flexed leg meant there would be no food, he began to actively stiffen the leg, to 'inhibit' the bending. After further learning '... we are almost able to raise the animal into the air by its extended limb' (Konorski, p. 227).

A less obvious kind of inhibition of responding can be attributed to the NO-GO stimulus in a successive discrimination. It may be related to frustration, or aversive emotional state, since the NO-GO stimulus serves as a negative reinforcer; furthermore, tranquillizing drugs often 'release' the inhibition, so that the formerly prohibited responses are made once more. Pavlov's procedure for producing stimuli which were 'conditioned inhibitors' (p. 38) continues to be used to demonstrate that a negative stimulus may continue to inhibit responding when combined with a positive stimulus (Hearst *et al.*, 1970).

A phenomenon which was initially predicted on the basis of a theory of inhibition is the change in preference for positive stimuli produced by discrimination training. *Peak shift* (Purtle, 1973) occurs when the peak of a generalization gradient (cf. Fig. 8.1) is shifted away from a negative stimulus. For instance if a line pointing north-east is used as the 'correct' stimulus, but a line pointing north-west is the 'wrong' cue, a generalization test with lines pointing to sixteen points of the compass might show that east by north-east, is the 'most-preferred' inclination. The idea is that the inhibition of the 'wrong' westerly cue has pushed the point of preference even further in the 'correct' easterly direction. An experiment like this with seven- to eleven-year-old children suggested that peak shift was a sign of emotional immaturity (Nicholson and Gray, 1972) but it has been found in adults for some tasks and is regularly obtained with animals.

A phenomenon often found under the same conditions as peak shift is *behavioural contrast*, which is an exaggeration of responding to the positive stimulus when it is intermingled with less favourable or negative situations. Vast amounts of research have so far failed to make very much sense of this, perhaps because there are several different reasons why response rates to a discriminative stimulus should be elevated (Mackintosh, 1974). But on the whole it is a fairly safe guess that mixing-up 'good' conditions with 'less-good' or 'bad' periods for the same individual enhances value or effectiveness of the 'good' circumstances. The trials of adversity may make one more appreciative of an otherwise unrelieved sufficiency. The adversities imposed in animal experiments have included absent or less frequent food rewards, more difficult tasks to obtain food rewards, reduced intensities of rewarding brain stimulation or the addition of electric shocks. Exposure to these 'hardships' has often produced more enthusiastic responding in subsequent standard conditions.

It is not clear that all the different ways of reducing the attractiveness of the situation should be regarded as producing a single kind of 'inhibition', but they point up the fact that 'not responding' to the negative stimulus in a simple discrimination may be accompanied by an unpleasant emotional state. Is this strictly necessary? Both Skinner (1938) and more recently Terrace (1966) have thought that the typical discrimination learning experiment makes the task more difficult than it need be by first training the subject to respond to the negative stimulus $(S-)$ and then requiring him to go into reverse. Surely one could train the subject not to respond to the 'wrong' stimulus in the first place? This, it turns out, produces faster learning of the discrimination task, with very few mistakes, and fewer unpleasant emotional consequences, as far as can be assessed by the absence of peak-shift and behavioural contrast. The techniques needed for this 'errorless discrimination learning' are:

(a) never reinforce responses to $S-$ from the start of training; (b) introduces $S-$ early in training, before there is much tendency for the subject to respond to it by generalization; (c) *fade-in* the $S-$ gradually, starting with short exposures and low intensities; (d) for a difficult discrimination, start off with an easy task and then fade-in the difficult discrimination by superimposing it on the easier task.

These results indicate that 'inhibitory' emotional states are not a necessary concomitant of discrimination learning, or of a sustained or very well learned discrimination. If, however, discriminations are established by associating one stimulus with 'good' outcomes and another with 'bad', it is not surprising that early stages of learning are accompanied by a variety of emotional effects.

Attending and not-attending

The inhibition concept applies to the control of response output – Konorski's dog stiffened its leg to inhibit the movement of bending, and the definition of inhibition requires withholding of response. Equally important, but more difficult to measure, is the modulation of stimulus input, which is roughly what is meant in this context by *attention* (see also A4). The subject's external methods of control of stimulus input are easy enough to observe – opening and closing of eyes, direction of gaze, eye movements etc – but it is assumed that selection of different aspects of the environment can go on in the absence of such outward signs. 'Paying attention' to colour rather than shape, or listening for the sound of high-pitched but not low-pitched tones may have little effect on the movements of looking or listening. Whether or not 'attention' is actually happening has therefore to be deduced rather than directly observed.

The complete learning of a discrimination generally implies both that the attention is being paid to the correct stimuli and that the responses are being directed accordingly. Complications arise because there are many degrees of correct analysis of stimuli and degrees of response restriction. You may walk on the grass *either* because you have misunderstood the sign which says 'Keep off' *or* you are walking in spite of having correctly read the sign. Conceivably you have carefully avoided looking at the sign *in case* it says 'Keep off'. Possibilities similar to this make interpretation of discrimination learning in terms of attentional processes rather speculative, but some progress has been made in designing experiments which distinguish changes in attention from changes in response output.

Some stimuli get more attention than others
This is one way in which attentional processes are fairly obvious. Strong reinforcing stimuli such as shock or food are not likely to be ignored, but some aspects of discriminative stimuli command immediate attention, irrespective of reward and punishment. For many animals smells are 'more important' than sights or sounds, and discriminations based on smells may more easily be learned than those based on the visual sense (p. 112. Bright colours on the other hand may more readily be attended to than shapes or sounds in some species; this seems to be true of the pigeon. Pigeons given food for pecking a yellow key 'notice' the yellowness, to the extent that they tend to stop pecking if the colour is changed (Fig. 8.1). If a similar experiment is done using sound, with a note of top C sounded instead of the yellow colour, the top C is ignored in that the birds carry on pecking in exactly the same way if the pitch of the tone is changed considerably in either direction (Jenkins and Harrison, 1960). By and large, vivid or intense stimuli will attract more attention from any species, but it has been proposed that each species could have its own stimulus preferences. Innate factors necessarily at least place limits on stimulus input, in the sense that animals with no colour receptors will be insensitive to colour. Even more detailed aspects of shape perception are built in to the nervous system (Hubel and Weisel, 1963) and therefore it is possible that certain shapes, or types of movement, are particularly vivid for a particular species.

However, sensitivity to types of stimuli can certainly be modified by experience. Conditioning factors can produce short-term changes in attention value of particular stimuli or stimulus categories (see below). Another kind of environmental influence, which may produce irreversible changes in the way the brain deals with sensory information, is experience early in life. Kittens allowed to see only vertical stripes during the first months after birth are unable to play with sticks held horizontally because brain neurones sensitive to horizontal lines have not developed (Blakemore, 1973). Rats reared with lots of experience of circles and triangles are much better at discrimination problems using these shapes than others, so it may be that early experience has a great deal to do with perceptual abilities in later life.

Whether or not stimulus analysers are wired-in at birth or established by experience, it is possible that they will be sensitive to the motivational demands of the moment. It is likely that animals pay more attention to food when they are hungry than at other times and are alerted to any strange external stimulus by pain or danger (Bindra, 1969). Illness, as well as hunger, appears to predispose rats to notice tastes (p. 73). Effects such as these may have various causes, but it is convenient to summarize them by stating that the attention given to stimuli varies with their *importance*. The importance may change directly as a function of internal drives or more indirectly by the learning processes discussed in following sections. Diverse motivational effects are found in studies of human attention, including blocking of attention to obscene words, and enhanced sensitivity to the stimulus of one's own name (A4).

The effects of habituation and classical conditioning on attention

According to Sokolov (1963) it is possible for the conditioned response to become automatic after a time so that it is made with less 'attention' in this sense. On the whole, though, it is true to say that our attention to a stimulus declines as habituation progresses and increases during classical conditioning. But this meaning of 'attention', as similar to the orienting response, is not quite the same as *selective attention* which is the basis of a recent theory of discrimination learning (Sutherland and Mackintosh, 1971). The orienting reaction has more to do with alertness and arousal, or even awareness, produced by external stimuli, whereas selective attention deals with which aspect of a particular stimulus (for instance colour, shape or brightness) is perceived or processed. When you consider that there is yet another separate meaning of 'attention' – that of mental effort or concentration – it is less surprising that some psychologists try to avoid using the word altogether, by referring to 'stimulus control' instead.

Operant reinforcement for paying attention

The theory of Sutherland and Mackintosh (1971) is too complicated to be properly dealt with here but one of their basic assumptions is shared by a number of other theorists. This is the assumption that attention is paid to aspects of stimuli which are important while other aspects are ignored. Tests of this assumption can be made when what is important is the reinforcement in discrimination learning. The implication is that in all forms of discrimination learning, stimulus information of certain types is only processed for as long as the processing 'pays off' in terms of associations with reinforcement. In more specialized terms 'an analyser is strengthened when its outputs consistently make predictions about further events of importance to the animal' (Sutherland and Mackintosh, 1971). The selective utilization of certain aspects of stimulus displays is most obvious when animals are specifically trained to pay attention to different kinds of stimulus at different times, or to ignore some types of visual information. Reynolds (1961), for instance, trained pigeons to pay attention to the colour of a disc and ignore the shape of a superimposed shape some of the time, but the rest of the time to ignore colour and respond according to shape. The signal for which feature of the disc to attend to was given by the intensity of a side lamp. The method of training was to give reinforcements according to colour in one phase, but according to shape in the other. In a similar experiment, Ray (1969) first trained monkeys with separate stimuli. They had to press the left-hand lever if a vertical line was presented but the right-hand for a horizontal line, in the first problem. Then one of two colours were shown and they had to press left for red, but right for green. Now the monkeys were put in a situation of conflict, by presenting them with a *vertical* line on a *green* background. One stimulus told them to press right, and another to press left. The quandary could be resolved, because the rewards were obtained by pressing left for the green vertical display, but right for the red horizontal display. Tests showed that the monkeys accomplished this correct solution by ignoring the colours altogether and working on the basis of the vertical and horizontal lines, instead of learning that the colours now meant the opposite of their original training.

It seems as though dimensions or features such as colour, shape or angle can be 'switched in' or 'switched out' at will, given appropriate training. This is consonant with our expectations that we can instruct someone else to limit or expand their attention if we ask them to 'ignore the treble for a moment and listen to the resonance of the bass' or 'never mind the quality, feel the width'.

'Dimensions' and analysers. According to Piaget, it takes some time for children to 'pay attention' to physical dimensions such as volume, width and number in the right kind of way (C2) but we often assume that the environment can always be classified in terms of dimensions such as these, and in terms of other aspects of stimuli which we can verbally label, such as colour, angle, shape and so on. This is not justified, either with children or with animals. The behavioural justification of our statements that an animal is paying attention to colour, or a child is 'noticing how many there are', should depend on systematic tests, which reveal how the behaviour varies as function of variations in the physical stimuli (p. 104).

Even when we are sure that there is a close correspondence between a physical stimulus dimension, and a behavioural index of response, it may be difficult to tell exactly how the environmental information is being dealt with. A well-known example is the experiment by Lashley (1938) which showed that rats were discriminating between a square and a diamond shape. If rats are doing this it is tempting to assume that they are somehow 'seeing' the diamond and square in the same way that we do. Lashley found that his rats certainly weren't, in so far as they were not looking at the tops of the shapes at all, but only at the bottom, as became apparent when he presented the tops and bottoms separately. The physiological or perceptual theories of how a rat or a machine could discriminate between patterns such as the diamond and square deal with the *features* of the patterns that are processed – in Lashley's experiment, only the flat or pointed bottoms of the figures. *Analysers* are hypothetical mechanisms capable of picking out particular features (Sutherland and Mackintosh, 1971, and A4). It is worth remembering that focusing on one dimension of the same stimulus source – e.g. noticing a shape but ignoring its colour – is relatively difficult. On the other hand it is quite easy to switch attention *between* stimulus sources: closing your eyes to listen instead of look, or even listening with one ear rather than the other (Triesman, 1969).

Improved attention to a specific dimension. There are a number of reasons for believing that experience at learning some discrimination based on a particular dimension helps when it comes to learning another discrimination on the same dimension (Mackintosh, 1974). A simple way of showing this is to test

111

subjects with a series of problems using the same kind of stimuli to see if they show progressive improvements in learning ability. For instance, if monkeys first learn to choose a red object instead of a green one (to find food), then a black form not a blue, then an orange rather than a brown, they improve with each problem (Shepp and Schrier, 1969). They are becoming connoisseurs of colour, not merely adapting to the situation, since changing the relevant dimension of the objects *every time*, from colour to shape and back again, results in no improvement over the first few problems. It is possible that improved attention to a specific dimension, such as colour or brightness, is responsible when improvement in learning with a particular type of stimuli results from prolonged training on one pair of 'correct' and 'incorrect' cues (*overtraining*) or when the 'correct' and 'incorrect' cues are repeatedly reversed after the subject has learned them (*serial reversal learning*).

Non-specific improvements in attention. The best-known form of general improvement in learning ability with experience is the *learning set* phenomenon (Harlow, 1949). This was discovered in a series of experiments with monkeys like the Shepp and Schrier one just mentioned. If rhesus monkeys are given several hundred problems, of choosing one from two objects presented to them, they learn increasingly quickly until, when presented with a new pair of objects, it only takes them one or two trials to find out which is the right one. It is as if they were able to say after the first trial '*this* is the right one' if they chose correctly, or '*the other one* is the right one' if they had picked the wrong one. When subjects show this ability to make any new choice, they are sometimes said to have learned a *win-stay lose-shift strategy* (Mackintosh, 1974). Some results apparently confirm estimates that rats, cats and different kinds of monkey can be placed on an ascending scale of 'learning set ability'. Although a battery of learning tasks would probably confirm this ranking, it probably depends over much on visual skills, since rats have demonstrated rapid formation of learning sets when choices between two smells have to be learned (Slotnick and Katz, 1974). Perhaps learning sets are not quite so non-specific as we think and the monkeys are not so much 'learning to think' as 'learning what to look for'. Although it is less generally useful, other animals with poor vision may be able to 'learn what to smell for'.

112

While 'knowing what to look for' can make all the difference in some tasks it is really more like a specialized perceptual skill than a general increase in 'attentiveness'.

Narrowing of attention span. In so far as attention corresponds to what we mean by being aware of a stimulus, or concentrating on a particular cue, it is usually accepted that we can only 'attend to one thing at a time'. This is not really to say that nothing else is learned or remembered apart from the thing attended to, but it is usually easier to learn 'one thing at a time'. This can be seen in conditioning experiments in the *overshadowing* and *blocking* of one stimulus by another. If two stimuli are given at the same time in a classical conditioning context, but one of them is 'better' than the other, animals often concentrate on the better one and ignore the other, as far as we can tell by separate tests. For example, a rather dim light might normally work perfectly well as a conditioned stimulus in a Pavlovian experiment (p. 36). But if a very loud buzzer is always sounded at the same time as the dim light is turned on, the buzzer may *overshadow* the light so that a dog does not salivate if the light is turned on by itself. Alternatively, if we used buzzers and lights of equivalent intensities, but trained the dog *first* with the buzzer, shining the light along with the buzzer might make very little impression on the animal, because listening carefully for the buzzer may *block* out attention to other stimuli (as happens when someone closes their eyes in order to listen more attentively).

The main point about narrowing of the attention span is the idea that there is a limit to our capacity to process information and attend to stimuli, which makes it necessary to cut down on attention to some sources in order to devote the maximum effort to the most important information (see A4). In-built salience, high intensity, novelty and past associations with reinforcement are all factors which seem to add to the 'importance' of particular stimulus categories. The activity of looking for or expecting a certain kind of feature, or of 'paying attention' more generally, is a very significant reflection of the importance of stimuli, apart from the avidity with which the information is processed once it is available. In this sense, the 'importance' of a stimulus can be assessed as the degree to which the stimulus reinforces the behaviour of attending.

Application of discrimination procedures – programmed learning.

Although discrimination learning is an area of considerable theoretical interest, the procedures and routines studied in this context are not without practical implications. Complex discriminations shade imperceptibly into concepts and cognitions, as we shall see in the next chapter; and rules of thumb which represent optimum conditions for successful discrimination learning have been found to provide useful guidelines in the design of the educational tools *programmed texts* and *computer assisted instruction* (Atkinson, 1968). Programmed texts are books in which the reader is invited to answer questions by writing in missing words as he goes along. This question-and-answer method is especially useful if the reader needs to memorize a good deal of the information in the book. Computer-assisted instruction is the latest form of the *teaching machines* advocated by Skinner. Simple teaching machines merely facilitate the presentation of the same type of material used in programmed texts, but a high technology version controlled by a computer may include batteries of coloured slides, light sensitive screens so that the student may register answers by 'pointing' to them with a special pen, and stereophonic headphones, not only for spoken instructions but also for the delivery of bursts of music as reinforcers.

Writing a programmed text or designing material for computer-assisted instruction requires at least as much skill and experience as traditional teaching, but there are several principles, dear to the hearts of behaviourists, which are generally adhered to.

(1) *Each individual proceeds at his own pace.* Few doubt that personal tuition has considerable advantages over group methods, and these are emphasized by an approach based on active learning. One-to-one training with a skilled teacher has yet to be superseded, but it is very entensive. Teaching machines and programmed texts are usually claimed to be cheaper, as well as better than their traditional equivalents. But it is essential that they are designed for individuals rather than groups.

(2) *Each individual makes active responses.* It is stressed that one should write in answers at every step of a programmed text. This insures that nothing is missed and leads to greater in-

114

volvement, like underlining or writing in the margin. It also allows for reinforcement of correct items. However even in computer-assisted instruction the responses are very restricted, compared with writing essays or 'learning by discovery' with miniature scientific or artistic projects. The argument is not that programmed learning should replace such alternatives, but rather that by taking care of the routine teaching jobs it releases more resources for additional goals.

(3) *Immediate reinforcement for correct learning.* Immediate and frequent reinforcement by 'getting it right' should lead to more accurate learning, since students cannot 'get hold of the wrong end of the stick' and carry on regardless. It should also add incentive to the task. Further incentives include an interesting and colourful presentation of material, including the use of puppets and cartoon characters in some cases. 'Playing with the machine' may be an additional reinforcer with the computer-controlled consoles.

Reinforcement should be *positive*, not negative or punishing, as far as possible: 'getting it right' can be encouraged but 'getting it wrong' should *not* be penalized. Children disparaged for getting their sums wrong are less likely to try to get them right than they are to dislike both sums and the teacher (or machine) which does the disparaging.

(4) *Minimizing errors.* Discriminations are less painful if they can be accomplished without errors. This contradicts the truism that we 'learn by our mistakes' and some programmes called *branching* or *intrinsic* are designed not so much to minimize mistakes as to provide remedial sub-routines for different types of mistake. In programmed texts this is rarely possible, and a *linear* type of programme is used, which breaks down the material into extremely small and easy steps. If very small steps are used, and easy concepts are established before being elaborated into more difficult ones, few errors need be made, and the student progresses in an atmosphere of success. The ideal programme allows more gifted students to go through fast without getting bored, but provides ample time and material to ensure that slower learners do not get discouraged. Many linear programmes are very much spoonfeeding operations, but it is valuable to have spoonfeeding that works, since more challenging undertakings can always be added.

On the whole, programmed texts and teaching machines have had a limited impact on educational practices. However, the basic idea of trying to make learning easier and more enjoyable is still gaining ground (C5) and advancing technology may mean that the computer-assisted teaching machine eventually becomes commonplace.

Summary and conclusions

Learning a discrimination implies that we learn to perceive the difference between two similar things, and that we also learn to make separate responses to the two cases. Recent theories assume that perceptual learning and response learning are distinct from one another. The perceptual kind may involve learning to be alert and learning to pay attention to particular aspects of events such as colour or shape. Response learning frequently requires the inhibition of responses because the task demands that responses are not given to the incorrect stimulus. The practical techniques which bring about discrimination learning, and which may profitably be adapted for use in educational aids, are dominated by the need to associate reinforcement with a limited set of stimuli.

9
Concept learning: reinforcement for abstract behaviour

Can speech, thought and imagination be reinforced and learned like other behaviours? The behaviourist tradition says yes, up to a point (Ch. 1). Sechenov's 100-year-old slogan, 'all acts of conscious or unconscious life are reflexes', is in fact more deterministic than modern behaviourist analyses which include such concepts as 'self-generated stimulus control' and 'commitment'. But one can still defend Darwin's belief that even the faculties of speech and imagination, which seem to set humans apart, are elaborations of abilities already present in lower species (see A7). It is reasonable to take the view that what is special about human language and thought is not that they are immune from general processes of learning and reinforcement, but that they are uniquely sensitive to these influences. Despite the reasonableness of this view, the reader will be aware that it is a matter of controversy (C2, A7). The tendency for human beings to talk to each other in a highly systematic and relatively meaningful fashion probably depends on innate propensities as much as social pressures and cultural conventions. Linguists since Chomsky (1959) have become convinced that no-one would have either the inclination or capacity to speak grammatically if it were not for innate propensities, while behaviourists have always stressed the importance of upbringing, training and individual experience in verbal as in all behaviour (Skinner, 1957). A nature-nurture debate has raged for the last fifteen years, and seems to be dying down without any satisfactory compromise, but both sides are now well aware of the contradictions inherent in either extreme view (A7).

Although the language problem in its own right has been the major focus of argument, it also represents to some extent the wider issue of the uniqueness of man (F7). Apart from language, there is an almost endless list of psychological attributes which distinguish man from humbler beasts: moral sense; tool-using; foresight; self-consciousness; sense of beauty – these were the kind of characteristics which Darwin felt he had to deal with (Ch. 1). Neither Darwin nor contemporary behavioural psychologists require that we ignore or forget these human traits; rather, they urge us to remember that human behaviour has evolved both biologically and culturally. Therefore, psychological principles which are *not* uniquely human may apply to uniquely human behaviours.

Three kinds of activity which are especially rather than uniquely human, where a behavioural analysis can be attempted, are the discrimination of stimulus concepts, learning by imitation, and learning to communicate with signs and symbols.

Discrimination of stimulus concepts

The term 'concept' can be applied to classes of objects, such as 'chairs', 'blue ribbons', 'tall trees'; to complicated physical dimensions like 'space', 'time' and 'infinity'; and to abstract ideas, as in the 'concept of democracy'. Used so broadly, it covers almost all intelligent activity, especially in the context of Piaget's theories (C2). There is a case for distinguishing the several kinds, and I want to concentrate on an elementary sort which I have termed *stimulus concepts*, to emphasize that discriminations on the grounds of stimulus attributes alone is the criterion. Stimulus concepts in this sense can be defined as discriminations which work for very large numbers of individual stimuli (Ch. 8). If a monkey learns to pick out blue objects of various sizes from a wide choice of colours, there are grounds for saying that the monkey has 'acquired the concept of blue objects', although it is a lot simpler to say that he is picking out blue objects.

The theoretical question is whether the monkey is responding merely on the basis of perceptual similarity of the objects, or because he has attained an underlying 'abstract' idea of blueness (A7). In the case of colour it is difficult to see what difference it makes. However there are some stimulus concepts that are clearly *about* stimuli, but are abstract in so far as they are not about *particular* stimuli. Examples of these are the concepts of oddity, similarity and regularity of stimulus objects.

Oddity. If three or more objects are presented at the same time, one can be different from the others in shape, colour, size or in several ways at once. If a new set of things is shown at each occasion for choice, the only way of always choosing the 'odd' one is by the abstract principle of oddness, rather than by perceptual similarity *per se*. Monkeys and apes can solve oddity problems quite well and rats and pigeons can occasionally, with some difficulty, achieve similar solutions, if the right kind of cues are used. This suggests that we should consider 'abstract-ness' as a matter of degree, and not an all-or-nothing condition. Rats may learn to choose the odd stimulus, whatever it is, in the domain of smells, without being able to transfer the rule to visual stimuli. Monkeys and men have similar capacities for generalizing the 'oddity' principle within several visual dimensions (Bernstein, 1961) but monkeys probably could not apply the rule across modalities – from visual displays to sounds for instance – as well as people.

Similarity. In theory, if an animal can point to the 'odd' one of a collection of objects it can also indicate the 'similar' ones. A technique for getting at this perception of similarity is the 'matching-to-sample' procedure (p. 103). In pioneering work in the 1920s, a chimpanzee was simply given a sample and required to pick a similar object from a tray. A common pro-cedure nowadays is to use three displays, with a middle one containing the sample, so that the animal is rewarded if it cor-rectly indicates which of the two outer displays is more similar to the middle one. Pigeons and monkeys can match up colours or shapes in this procedure, though here again pigeons appear to acquire a lesser degree of abstractness than monkeys. Novel colours are sometimes not matched properly by pigeons, and they match some shapes better than others. Rhesus monkeys, on the other hand, can learn a 'rule' of matching for simi-larity which generalizes to entirely new objects, even after damage to the frontal lobes of the brain (Mishkin *et al.*, 1962). Pigeons can do very well at judging new colours in terms of their similarity to familiar standards (Wright and Cumming, 1969), but this might be construed as more perceptual than abstract as the judgements relate to the limited domain of the familiar standards.

Regularity. It now becomes necessary to make a very obscure distinction between 'perceptual abstraction' and 'non-perceptual abstraction'. This is because some theorists, such as Sutherland (1968), believe that perception itself requires forming and storing fairly abstract rules about sensory features. Sutherland's abstract rules work just to accomplish pattern recognition for one set of stimuli, and do not *necessarily* produce generalization of concepts to entirely new sets of stimuli, or to new modalities. But these perceptual abstractions add further weight to the notion of continuity between discrimination and stimulus concepts.

The perception of regularities and repeated motifs demonstrates existence of perceptual rules. Rats trained to distinguish between a regular checkerboard pattern and one with a particular 'mistake' such as an extra black square can generalize the concept of 'regular v. irregular' to many other pairs of patterns differing widely from the originals (Sutherland and Williams, 1969). Even goldfish tend to generalize from a single square with a bump on the top to one with a notch in place of the bump, again presumably on the basis of the 'abstract' coding of a discontinuity or irregularity. It is very difficult therefore to draw a hard and fast line between generalization on the basis of perceptual similarity and generalization on the basis of abstract principles, because so much of perception requires a degree of abstraction (see A4 and A7).

There is an obvious need to differentiate the stimulus concepts possessed by goldfish from those we use ourselves, but it may be that verbal labels we apply to concepts, and the thoughts we have about them, are a lot more important than the process of perceptual analysis in giving our concepts their 'higher' properties. An example to think about is the efficiency of the stimulus concept of 'people' used by pigeons. When shown a large collection of holiday slides, some showing people and some not, pigeons have no difficulty in distinguishing scenes which contain people from those which do not, although the images of people have little in common as the holiday slides have shown people of various ages, at different distances and angles, wearing clothes and not wearing clothes and so on (Herrnstein and Loveland, 1964). This is a reminder that most animals have to be capable of categorizing information in a fairly abstract way into concepts such as 'dog' 'perching place' and 'close to home' in order to operate outside the laboratory. As a counterpart to this, we might note that we become capable of using quite difficult concepts perceptually 'at a glance'.

Learning by imitation

One of the many unresolved theoretical problems in the analysis of learning is whether or not learning comes in distinct types. Gagne (1965) following Tolman (1932; see Ch. 1) lists eight separate types, starting with classical and operant conditioning and ending with concept learning and problem solving. It is safe to say that we really know very little about the brain processes that bring about one sort of learning, let alone eight different sorts, but it is difficult to avoid some speculation based on the existence of different procedures for learning different sorts of things. Hence the questions of whether operant conditioning differs from classical conditioning, or whether concept learning differs from discrimination learning. Although these particular enigmas are rather esoteric there is a similar but more obvious question of whether it matters if you learn by watching somebody else as opposed to doing it yourself. On the face of it, learning to ride a bicycle is based on a certain amount of trial and error on the part of the rider, but watching someone else first probably helps and hints about which way to turn the handle-bars might cut down on some of the errors in the 'trial and error'. Using the most up-to-date techniques, we could also facilitate learning by showing the trainee bike rider a videotape – if necessary in slow-motion – of his own mistakes and successes. The problem for learning theory is that there are an infinite number of kinds of situation in which learning can take place, and almost as many 'methods of instruction' as there are teachers. It isn't very satisfactory to say that there is a different 'type' of learning produced in each case. Gagne's solution is probably as good as any, for the time being, with differences between being told what to do, taking notes from lectures, watching videotapes and so on, coming under the heading of different 'media for instruction'. But we might look for major divisions between learning by doing, learning by watching, and learning via language.

Of course if we include listening, smelling etc, along with watching, we have a very general category of learning by stimulus input that would include habituation and classical conditioning (which can take place perfectly well under paralysis). But the main thing about watching and listening is that they include the possibility of learning by *imitation* or, as it is termed by Bandura, *modelling* (see B1). Bandura (1973) has been particularly interested in the imitation of violent and aggressive behaviour, but imitation of non-violence is equally important (see C1). Imitation of non-fearful or non-neurotic behaviour has also been studied intensively, and is a valuable facet of some forms of behaviour modification (Bandura, 1969, and Ch. 2). Children who are afraid of dogs may be reassured if another child 'shows how' a dog can be patted without harm; students who are mildly phobic about snakes can become less afraid of them after watching films of other students handling snakes, as part of a desensitization procedure (see Ch. 3). In all forms of 'learning by imitation' interpretation is complicated by the presence of further 'sub-types' of influence on behaviour. 'Parrot-fashion' mimicry, or copying of response skills, is often combined with either short-term or long-term emotional links between the observer and the observed person, or *model*. In the short-term it may be a matter of *social facilitation* of reinforced behaviours. (It is well known that when the main character in a film lights up a cigarette, smokers in the audience reach for their own pack.) This is usually regarded as an elementary process since chickens, whose intellect is not of the highest order, are extremely susceptible and will eat merely because others are eating. A similar effect has been demonstrated in rats who are also highly aroused by observing the sexual activities of other rats. Probably most social animals are sensitive to the actions and emotional states of others in their group, through a variety of mechanisms.

In the case of human personality development, there is a tendency to 'identify' emotionally with parents or heroes so that 'being like X' becomes a reinforcer. In this case the status of X has considerable significance. Status may be acquired by being a 'nurturant' figure, that is by giving comfort and other necessities to the observer. The parent-child relationship is the obvious one, but imitation of authority figures like concentration camp guards has also been put in this category. Alternatively a model acquires status by receiving or possessing strong reinforcers – a hero (or heroine) with conspicuous riches, fame or talent may be imitated because his hairstyle or attitudes are associated with such powerful rewards. Bandura's work has shown that there is much to be gained by separate consideration of the effects of reinforcers obtained by the model, and direct reinforcers given to the observer for imitating a model.

Imitation as a response class can be encouraged in children by giving reinforcers such as approval or sweets after particular instances of imitation (Baier and Sherman, 1964), and this is an effective tool in remedial education. Copying of sounds or movements often appears to occur spontaneously, however, and may function as an intrinsically reinforcing activity at some stages of human development. Experiments in which animals learn the standard operant response of bar-pressing either by watching another animal or by conventional methods (Ch. 1) suggest that some kind of copying of movements is readily obtainable in rats, and is a superior training method for cats, at least if the observer and model cats are friends (John *et al.*, 1968). The chimpanzee Washoe (see p. 127) learned some gestures by imitation, although it was not the optimal training method.

Imitation can be regarded therefore as a mode of learning, and an influence on the performance of already learned behaviours, which can be affected by experience and reinforcement in various ways. There is marked discrepancy between the importance ascribed to imitation in the development of personality and social behaviours (see B1, C3) and the low esteem in which imitation is held by many psychologists who study the growth of thought and language in children (C2). This may reflect the ease with which personal mannerisms and emotional reactions can be acquired, compared with the more demanding tasks required in cognitive development. It appears, however, that imitation can assist the learning of cognitive skills by children in experimental settings. A review by Zimmerman and Rosenthal (1974) deals with language skills, which I shall mention in the next section, and also concept attainment. Stimulus concepts needed to pick out cards with certain combinations of dots and squiggles on them can be learned by watching someone else sort the cards. More important for educational practice is the finding that the more abstract 'Piagetian' type of concept can also be learned by observation. The best-known example is the 'conservation' problem, in which a four- or five-year-old has to learn that orange juice, say, poured from a short fat glass into a tall thin glass stays the same instead of becoming 'more' because it comes up higher in the thin glass. Learning to imitate friends who say it's 'the same' may be another of the many factors which affect children's answers (and 'cognitive processes') in this situation. Watching another child respond correctly to one conservation task not only helps children get that particular one right, but also improves their judgement of other conservation problems.

Learning with words

There are two aspects of learning with words that have particularly attracted the attention of psychologists. The first is learning that takes place when adults read, and the second that which occurs when babies learn to talk. A great deal of specialized work has been done in both areas and it is covered in A6, A7 and C2 of this series. I shall confine myself to a brief foray into the linguist/behaviourist battle over the nature of language and words.

For brevity and point the contemporary behaviourist view of learning to talk espoused in 1940 by Bertrand Russell cannot be bettered:

> In learning to speak, there are two elements, first, the muscular dexterity, and second, the habit of using a word on appropriate occasions. We may ignore the muscular dexterity, which can be acquired by parrots. Children make many articulate sounds spontaneously, and have an impulse to imitate the sounds made by adults. When they make a sound which the adults consider appropriate to the environment, they find the results pleasant. Thus, by the usual pleasure-pain mechanism which is employed in training performing animals, children learn, in time, to utter noises appropriate to objects that are sensibly present, and then, almost immediately, they learn to use the same noises when they desire the objects ... (Russell, 1940, p. 69)

Skinner's view of language. Skinner's analysis of verbal behaviour (1957) is essentially an elaboration and extension of earlier behaviourist treatments. Russell's interpretation was not behaviourist enough for Skinner, as Russell adds a certain amount of introspection and mental imagery. Skinner's approach is more radical because it excludes *any* non-behavioural factors like mental images, thoughts or cognitions as explanations for what is said or written. This is not a denial that people do or feel the things normally referred to as 'thoughts' or 'images', but a hypothesis that these can be taken as a special category of behaviour itself rather than a 'higher' or 'deeper' source. Although this is a difficult hypothesis to support, since it flies in the face of common belief, not all of what Skinner says is at variance with facts accepted by others. The division of speech into utterances for naming, commenting and requesting seems inevitable, and Skinner found it convenient to term the first two *tacts* (for 'makes contact with') and the third *mands* (for 'demand'). It has been confirmed that the early speech of infants consists largely of simple comments and requests, although it has proved extremely hard to determine to what extent these are influenced by the support of those caring for the child, as opposed to the intrinsic satisfactions of making comments and requests (Brown, 1973; see C2).

Skinner deals extensively with literary devices and figures of speech, and includes a behavioural interpretation of parts of *Finnegans Wake*. Conversation, the recall of memorized verbal material and the skills of translation are subsumed under the heading of *intraverbal* responses, while certain organizing relations between words, including the rules of grammar, are singled out as *autoclitic processes* (see A7). The central theme is not a linguistic analysis of language, but the accumulation of support for the proposition that what we say and write is determined by the environment rather than spontaneous inspiration or intuition. The environment, however, includes our past and present experience, education, culture, purpose and audience.

Chomsky's view of language. Chomsky's opinion is precisely the opposite of Skinner's, as he feels that the environment, however construed, has an almost negligible influence on the nature of language, or on knowledge generally. Liebniz's remarkable suggestion that even arithmetic and geometry are all in the mind to start with is quoted with approval by Chomsky, who takes the position that language learning is a matter of 'drawing out what is innate in the mind' (Chomsky, 1965, pp. 50–51). Even when language itself has been drawn out we cannot actually give information about verbal ambiguities to someone by telling him of them 'but simply arrange matters in such a way that his linguistic intuition, previously obscured, becomes evident to him' (Chomsky, 1965, p. 22). This seems as much a contradiction of common sense as Skinner's radical hypothesis but is not an essential feature of the more moderate Chomskyan view, that the character of language as a grammatical form is a product of innate predispositions rather than cultural invention or individual experience.

The distinction between the 'ideal knowledge' or *competence* for a language, and the realities of actual speech or *performance*, make it difficult to apply Chomsky's theories to practical situations (see A7). Since actually speaking or writing is not really part of the theory, except as a pale reflection of ideal linguistic knowledge, there is not much to say about any linguistic performance, in particular that of the fairly large numbers of individuals who have speech impediments or difficulties in learning to read and write (see C5, F2). Chomsky (1965, p. 58) is concerned with something that is independent of 'intelligence, motivation, and emotional state' and comes entirely from *inside* the individual. Skinner's hypothesis at least gives those on the outside something to do to help, and the evidence suggests that it works (Yule *et al.*, 1974, and see p. 60). Part of Chomsky's argument against a theory of language based on learned discriminations is that a sentence such as 'The W Xed the Y in the Z' can be recognized as grammatical in principle even though it bears little similarity, as a superficial stimulus, to any real or meaningful sentence. Chomsky offers a theory of grammar which is independent of particular meanings or words, and can therefore explain why we can understand and say completely novel sentences, and judge whether they are grammatical or not. He has pointed out, however, (1965, p. 148) that a number of specialized rules have to be added to this basic theory of grammar to explain why some grammatical sentences make more sense than others. In areas like this a more behaviourist theory has some advantages. Consider for example these two sentences in the form just mentioned: 'The government overpaid the universities in the crisis'; 'The opposite appeared the safer in the sky'. The first is nonsensical from bitter experience rather than grammatical criteria. The second needs some grammatical analysis to identify why 'appeared' here is not an action, while 'overpaid' in the first sentence is. But a straightforward conditioning theory ought to be able to explain why 'circumstances' is a more acceptable word than 'sky'.

Obviously I do not share Chomsky's conviction that ordinary behavioural principles have nothing to do with language. Although Chomsky's theorizing has dominated most psychological discussion of language for some time, few psychologists have been prepared to abandon behavioural investigation altogether, and there is a vast spectrum of ideas about language between the polar extremes of Chomsky and Skinner (see A7 and C2). Apart from the usefulness of imitation and reinforcement in remedial training of language skills in people, evidence that learned discriminations may contribute to methods of communication in animals has some bearing on the issue.

Language skills in animals
The ability of some birds to mimic human speech remains fascinating, but is being overshadowed by the competence of chimpanzees in some forms of artificial communication. However, a monograph by Marler (1970) did suggest some points of similarity between vocal learning in birds and language acquisition in children. In some species it is necessary for the young first to hear the appropriate song-pattern, and then to take time to develop their own vocal ability to match the remembered sounds. This is an example where early 'models' of sound production are important, even if imitation does not take place immediately. Since children talk in a different manner from surrounding adults the value of imitation in language learning has been discounted (C2). But by analogy with Marler's birds it may be the case that children's ability to reproduce speech lags behind their capacity to perceive it. The finding that imitation may serve in the acquisition of rule-governed speaking and understanding has enhanced current interest in this kind of possibility (Zimmerman and Rosenthal, 1974).

Washoe's gestures. Several attempts to teach chimpanzees to speak have got no further than two or three recognizable grunts. Human speech requires specialized vocal apparatus which chimps do not have. It is a distinct possibility that the vocal apparatus necessary for speech sounds appeared at the very last stage of human evolution, when homo sapiens replaced neanderthal man (Lieberman, 1974). But we have since then invented numerous forms of communication that do not depend on speech – pictographic writing and bookmakers' tic-tac among them. It now looks as though chimpanzees have the intellectual capacity to make intelligent use of some of these non-speech systems. Several chimps have successfully been trained to use signs in the American Sign Language (ASL) in which signs represent words rather than letters. Chimpanzees in the wild are accustomed to using gestures in social interaction, but Washoe and other chimps who learn ASL are taught the names of objects like toothbrush, cat, doll. New signs are taught by imitation, prompting and reinforcement (Ch. 4), and teachers and human companions often use ASL between themselves. Washoe was the first chimp trained by the Gardners (1969) who are now repeating their success with some newborn chimps. (Washoe was six-months old before language training was started.) Her accomplishments include using about 100 separate signs such as *drink*, *up*, *baby*, *help*, *hurry*, and several hundred two- and three-sign combinations, from *more tickle*, to *hurry open door*, many being of her own invention. One recent story is that she used the sign *dirty* taught to her during toilet training, to describe an unfriendly rhesus monkey – perhaps chimpanzees can acquire not only language, but bad language (Fleming, 1975).

Sarah's thoughts. Washoe's gesturing was very like human language in the sense of social speech, but did not contain much evidence of academic ability. It was play-talk rather than school-talk, although Washoe was given tests to make sure she could 'name' objects and pictures of objects correctly. Sarah was a six-year-old 'adolescent' before she began two years of intensive training designed by Premack (1970) to teach a range of intellectual skills. Communication is achieved by physical tokens, rather than by gestures or speech, which are used in a one hour per day training session, rather than being a permanent part of life. Different words such as *banana, bucket, insert, same, different, yes, no* are represented by distinctive pieces of plastic, varying in shape size and colour. These plastic 'words' are metal-backed, so that they can be 'written' by experimenter or chimp, by laying them out on a magnetized board. Step-by-step discrimination training, using mainly the positive reinforcers of attractive foods, enabled Sarah to demonstrate several skills normally associated with language. First, she followed instructions of the type *Sarah insert banana pail apple dish*, spelled out in the plastic words. Second, she answered questions about objects by 'writing' *yes* or *no* or filling in blanks. For instance, real objects like an apple and a car key were shown along side a word which meant *same as*, with a word for *question mark*, and Sarah answered by replacing the *question mark* with *no*. Thirdly, this technique was used for more abstract concepts, including the concept of *name*. Given the words *red is question apple* Sarah could answer *colour of*. If she was given *apple is question* with a real apple, Sarah selected the answer *name of*. The function of the 'word' as a symbol for the real object is demonstrated by using the blue triangle which means apple to ask questions like *question colour of apple*, getting the answer *red*. Even though the 'word' itself was a blue triangle, Sarah said that it was round and red.

Premack concludes: 'The procedures that train animals will also produce words'. Obviously the plastic words are not the 'same as' spoken or printed words, as Sarah would undoubtedly tell us if we asked her. The very difference probably accounts for one of the practical applications of Premack's language system, which is to provide a means of communication for individuals who cannot use normal language, either because they have never learned, or because they have had an accident which has damaged speech centres in the brain. Symbols exactly like Sarah's have been learned by children unable to talk normally. The plastic words are probably a lot easier to learn than normal reading and writing, and may be easier than speech for some children. A system that depends on vision is obviously useful for anyone with problems of vocal production or hearing. A more mysterious possibility is that the artificial communication systems bring into play different parts of the brain from natural human speech – a patient who could not comprehend or produce written or spoken words properly after removal of 'speech areas' on the left side of the brain has been trained to a higher level than Sarah with a system of pictures drawn on index cards (Baker *et al.*, 1975).

Lana's sentences. The day-to-day living quality of Washoe's communicating and the academic correctness of Sarah's grammar have been combined in the system taught to another girl chimp, Lana (Rumbaugh *et al.*, 1973). She has a console like a large typewriter keyboard on which she can type requests to a computer twenty-four hours a day, as well as use for exchanging messages with her trainer during his visits. Signs on the keys are in the artificial language 'Yerkish', invented for this purpose, which uses combinations of nine stimulus elements to make a rich variety of visual patterns or 'words'. Her keyboard is easier than a typewriter in that it has one 'word' per key, but more difficult in that the position of each word is varied randomly by the computer. The symbols on the keys which Lana pushes are 'written out' electronically on a display unit above the keyboard.

Training was by the usual step-by-step method with a variety of rewards. The computer could deliver bits of apple or banana and orange juice, play music and open the window. Tickling is a very powerful reinforcer for young chimpanzees and there was a symbol for tickling, although it had to be delivered by the human trainer rather than the machine. The first stage of training was to give apple, music and the rest whenever the appropriate keys were pressed. After this it did not take long for Lana to learn to string symbols together, progressing through the forms *please banana, please banana period* to *please machine give piece of banana period* and *please machine make window open period*. Pressing the period or full-stop key was a special response, because that was the signal for the computer to deliver the goods for a correct sentence or erase the message if words had been typed in an incorrect order. Sometimes Lana would press the *period* key halfway through a sentence to erase it and start again. This 'start again' function was used in a systematic test of whether Lana could tell the difference between 'grammatical' and 'ungrammatical' sentences. In testing sessions, some 'correct' sentences were half-written in for her on the display, e.g. *please machine give ...*, and Lana always completed the sentence to make up a particular request. But if some words were written up in a jumbled order, such as *please banana make ...*, Lana would reject these wrong words by pressing the *period* button and starting a new sentence.

It looks as though Lana has begun to recognize the order of words, in a first approximation to grammatical competence. This does not mean that she is ready for higher education, but it does add emphasis to the continuity between animal and human cognition. Lana's performance represents two other breakthroughs. The testing by computor avoids any possibility of 'Clever Hans' cueing from a human trainer (p. 104). Also the keyboard system seems to facilitate the asking of questions by the chimp. A question can be defined as a *mand*, or request, for information rather than objects. When Washoe asks *time eat?*, or a child makes a similar query, the request and the question boil down to the same thing. But the question becomes further removed from demand for an object when Lana asks *Tim give Lana name of this?* and Tim (her trainer) punches in the answer that it is called a box, before she asks if she can have the box

(Fleming, 1975). If reports like this are supported, and Premack's new work with dogs bears fruit (Premack, 1972), we may have to conclude that Darwin was right after all, and it is possible to communicate ideas to terriers (p. 11).

Summary and conclusions

Chomsky's position, that language can only be understood in terms of inborn human intuitions, and Skinner's, that a complete account of language and thought may be had from contingencies of reinforcement, are both extremes. A compromise will probably be necessary, but it cannot be said that any questions about language or concept learning have been firmly answered. However, the capacity for concept learning and communication in animals is proving to be substantial. Procedures for children which combine reinforcement techniques and imitation also suggest that the acquisition of rule-governed or abstract skills can be brought under the umbrella of a behaviourist approach to learning.

Thus the originally scandalous doctrines of behaviourism (Ch. 1), characterized by the intent to simplify complexities, can be defended on two counts. They continue to provide a down-to-earth base of methods and theory against which the wilder flights of psychological fancy can be tested. And, perhaps less expectedly, behaviourism in its modern forms has some claim to be a fertile source of recommendations for applied fields of human psychology.

Further reading

Books suitable for further reading in the References section are given an asterisk. Additional sources are listed here.

Books on learning and reinforcement

Hulse, S. H., Deese, J., and Egeth H. E. (1974) *The Psychology of Learning* (4th edn). New York: McGraw-Hill. Easy textbook.

Gray J. (1975) *Elements of a Two-Process Theory of Learning*. London: Academic Press. More difficult textbook (see also Mackintosh, 1974).

Millenson, J. R. (1967) *Principles of Behavioural Analysis*. London: Collier-Macmillan. Skinnerian textbook (see also Blackman, 1974, and Reynolds, 1968).

Application of behavioural principles

Kiernan, C. C. (1974) Behaviour modification. In A. M. Clarke and A. D. B. Clarke (eds) *Mental Deficiency: the changing outlook* (3rd edn). London: Methuen.

Staats, A. W. (1968) *Learning, Language and Cognition*. London: Holt, Rinehart and Winston.

Watson, L. S. (1973) *Child Behaviour Modification: a manual for teachers, nurses and parents*. Oxford: Pergamon.

Ulrich, R., Stachnik, T. and Mabry, J. (1966, 1970, 1974) *Control of Human Behaviour*, vols I, II and III. London: Scott Foresman. Substantial collections of readings, mostly clinical, but more on education in vol. III (see also Gagne, 1965, and Bandura, 1969).

References and
Name Index

Books suitable for further reading are marked with an asterisk

The numbers in italics following each reference refer to page numbers within this book.

Allyon, T. (1963) Intensive treatment of psychotic behaviour by stimulus satiation and food reinforcement. *Behaviour Research and Therapy* 1: 53–62. *30.*

Allyon, T. and Azrin, N. H. (1964) Instructions and reinforcement. *Journal of the Experimental Analysis of Behavior* 7: 327–31. *52*

Allyon, T. and Azrin, N. H. (1968) *The Token Economy*. New York: Appleton-Century-Crofts. *97*

Amsel, A. (1972) Behavioural habituation, counter conditioning and a general theory of persistence. In A. H. Black and W. F. Prokasy (eds) *Classical Conditioning, II*. New York: Appleton-Century-Crofts. *74, 86*

Atkinson, R. C. (1968) Computerized instruction and the learning process. *American Psychologist* 23: 225–39. *114*

Atkinson, R. C. and Wickens, T. D. (1971) Human memory and the concept of reinforcement. In R. Glaser (ed.) *The Nature of Reinforcement*. London: Academic Press. *101*

Azrin, N. H. and Holtz, W. C. (1966) Punishment. In W. K. Honig (ed.) *Operant Behaviour: Areas of Research and Application*. New York: Appleton-Century-Crofts. *71*

Azrin, N. H., Hutchinson, R. R. and Hake, D. F. (1966) Extinction-induced aggression. *Journal of the Experimental Analysis of Behaviour* 9: 191–204. *75*

Azrin, N. H., Sneed, T. J. and Foxx, R. M. (1974) Dry-bed training: rapid elimination of childhood enuresis. *Behavior Research and Therapy* 12: 147–56. *78*

Baer, D. M. and Sherman, J. A. (1964) Reinforcement control of generalized imitation in young children. *Journal of Experimental Child Psychology* 1: 37–49. *123*

Baker, E., Berry, T., Garner, A., Zurif, E., Davis, L. and Veroff, A. (1975) Can linguistic competence be dissociated from natural language functions? *Nature* 254: 509–10. *129*

*Bandura, A. (1969) *Principles of Behavior Modification.* New York: Holt, Rinehart and Winston. *122*

Bandura, A. (1973) *Aggression: A Social Learning Analysis.* London: Prentice Hall. *75, 122*

Barr, R. F. and McConaghy, N. (1972) A general factor of conditionability: A study of galvanic skin response and penile responses. *Behaviour Research and Therapy* 10: 215–227. *41*

Berlyne, D. E. (1969) The reward value of indifferent stimulation. In J. T. Tapp (ed.) *Reinforcement and Behavior.* New York: Academic Press. *27*

Bernstein, J. S. (1961) The utilization of visual cues in dimension-abstracted oddity by primates. *Journal of Comparative and Physiological Psychology* 54: 243–7. *119*

Bindra, D. (1968) Neuropsychological interpretation of the effects of drive and incentive-motivation on general activity and instrumental behaviour. *Psychological Review* 75: 1–22. *109*

*Blackman, D. (1974) *Operant Conditioning.* London: Methuen. *56*

Blakemore, C. (1973) Environmental constraints on development in the visual system. In R. A. Hinde and J. Stevenson-Hinde (eds) *Constraints on Learning.* London: Academic Press. *108*

Boe, E. E. and Church, R. M. (1967) Permanent effect of punishment during extinction. *Journal of Comparative and Physiological Psychology* 63: 486–92. *70*

Bolles, R. C. (1970) Species-specific defence responses and avoidance learning. *Psychological Review* 77: 32–48. *72*

Brady, J. V. (1958) Ulcers in 'executive monkeys'. *Scientific American* 199: 95–100.

Brener, J. (1973) Learned control of cardiovascular processes. In K. S. Calhoun, H. E. Adams and K. M. Mitchell (eds) *Innovative Treatment Methods in Psychopathology.* New York: John Wiley. *55*

Brown, P. L. and Jenkins, H. M. (1968) Auto-shaping of the pigeon's key peck. *Journal of the Experimental Analysis of Behavior* 11: 1–8. *50*

Brown, R. (1973) *A First Language.* London: George Allen and Unwin. *125*

Caggiula, A. R. (1970) Analysis of the copulation-reward properties of posterior hypothalamic stimulation in male rats. *Journal of Comparative and Physiological Psychology* 70: 399–412. *92*

Campbell, B. A. and Church, R. M. (1969) *Punishment and Aversive Behavior.* New York: Appleton-Century-Crofts. *69*

Castellucci, V., Pinsker, H., Kupferman, N. and Kandel, E. R. (1970) Neuronal mechanism of habituation and dishabituation of the gill withdrawal reflex in *Aplysia. Science* 167: 1745–8. *23*

Chomsky, N. (1959) Review of Skinner's *Verbal Behavior. Language* 35: 26–58. *112*

Chomsky, N. (1965) *Aspects of the Theory of Syntax*. Massachusetts: MIT Press. *125–6*

*Cofer, C. N. and Appley, M. H. (1964) *Motivation*. London: John Wiley. *100*

Crespi, L. P. (1942) Quantitative variation of incentive and performance in the white rat. *American Journal of Psychology 55*: 467–517. *57*

Crow, T. J. (1973) Catecholamine-containing neurones and electrical self-stimulation: 2. A theoretical interpretation and some psychiatric implications. *Psychological Medicine 3*: 66–73. *91*

Darwin, C. (1871) *The Descent of Man*. London: John Murray. *9–11, 19, 117, 118*

Davis, M. (1972) Differential retention of sensitization and habituation of the startle response in the rat. *Journal of Comparative and Physiological Psychology 78*: 210–67. *26*

Emmelkamp, P. M. G. and Wessels, H. (1975) Flooding in imagination vs flooding *in vivo*. *Behaviour Research and Therapy 13*: 7–15. *31*

Eysenck, H. J. (1973) *Eysenck on Extraversion*. London: Crosby, Lockwood and Staples. *29, 40*

Falk, J. L. (1972) The nature and determinants of adjunctive behavior. In R. M. Gilbert and J. D. Keehn (eds) *Schedule Effects: Drugs, Drinking and Aggression*. Toronto: University of Toronto Press. *100*

Ferster, C. B. (1961) Positive reinforcement and behavioural deficits of autistic children. *Child Development 32*: 437–56. *87*

Ferster, C. B. and Skinner, B. F. (1957) *Schedules of Reinforcement*. New York: Appleton-Century-Crofts. *47–50*

Fleming, J. (1975) The state of the apes. *Psychology Today 1*: 16–25. *128*

Foster, W. S., Walker, S. F. and Hurwitz, H. M. B. (1970) Effects of reinforcement on response alternation. *Psychonomic Science 19*: 171–3. *58*

*Gagné, R. M. (1965) *The Conditions of Learning*. New York: Holt, Rinehart and Winston. *121*

Gardner, R. A. and Gardner, B. T. (1969) Teaching sign language to a chimpanzee. *Science 165*: 664–72. *128*

Guttman, N. and Kalish, H. I. (1956) Discriminability and stimulus generalization. *Journal of Experimental Psychology 51*: 79–88. *104*

Harlow, H. F. (1949) The formation of learning sets. *Psychological Review 56*: 51–65. *112*

Harlow, H. F. (1958) The nature of love. *American Psychologist 13*: 673–85. *95*

Hearst, E., Besley, S. and Farthing, G. W. (1970) Inhibition and the stimulus control of operant behaviour. *Journal of the Experimental Analysis of Behavior 14*: 373–409. *105*

Heath, R. G. (1963) Electrical self-stimulation of the brain in man. *American Journal of Psychiatry 120*: 571–7. *89*

Herrnstein, R. J. (1969) Method and theory in the study of avoidance. *Psychological Review 76*: 46–69. *67–8*

Herrnstein, R. J. and Loveland, D. H. (1964) Complex visual concept in the pigeon. *Science 146*: 549–51. *120*

Herrnstein, R. J. and Loveland D. H. (1972) Food-avoidance in hungry pigeons, and other perplexities. *Journal of the Experimental Analysis of Behavior 18*: 369–83. *72*

*Hinde, R. A. (1970) *Animal Behaviour*. London: McGraw Hill. *23, 72, 74*

Hinde, R. A. (1972) *Nonverbal Communication*. Cambridge: Cambridge University Press. *95*

Hinde, R. A. and Stevenson-Hinde, J. (1973) *Constraints on Learning*. London: Academic Press. *47, 93*

Hodgson, R. J., Rachman, S. and Marks, I. M. (1972) The treatment of chronic obsessive compulsive neuroses: follow-up and further findings. *Behaviour Research and Therapy 10*: 181–9. *32*

Hoffman, H. S. and Ratner, A. M. (1973) A reinforcement model of imprinting: Implications for socialization in monkeys and men. *Psychological Review 80*: 527–44. *94*

Hubel, D. H. and Wiesel, T. N. (1963) Receptive fields of cells in the striate cortex of very young, visually inexperienced kittens. *Journal of Neurophysiology 26*: 994–1002. *108*

Hull, C. L. (1952) *A Behavior System*. New Haven: Yale University Press. *15, 21, 57*

Jenkins, H. M. (1973) Effects of the stimulus-reinforcer relation on selected and unselected responses. In R. A. Hinde and J. Stevenson-Hinde (eds) *Constraints on Learning*. London: Academic Press. *51*

Jenkins, H. M. and Harrison, R. H. (1960) Effect of discrimination training on auditory generalization. *Journal of Experimental Psychology 59*: 246–53. *108*

John, E. R., Chessler, F., Bartlett, F. and Victor, J. (1968) Observation learning in cats. *Science 159*: 1489–91. *123*

Kazdin, A. E. and Bootzin, R. R. (1972) The token economy: an evaluative review. *Journal of Applied Behavior Analysis 5*: 343–72. *97*

Kelleher, R. T. (1958) Fixed ratio schedules of conditioned reinforcement with chimpanzees. *Journal of the Experimental Analysis of Behavior 1*: 281–9. *98*

Kelleher, R. T. (1966) Conditioned reinforcement in second-order schedules. *Journal of the Experimental Analysis of Behavior 9*: 475–85. *98*

Konorski, J. (1948) *Conditioned Reflexes and Neuron Organization*. Cambridge: Cambridge University Press. *105*

Lashley, K. S. (1938) The mechanism of vision. XV: Preliminary studies of the rat's capacity for detail vision. *Journal of General Psychology 18*: 123–93. *111*

Lieberman, P. (1974) *On the Origins of Language: An Introduction to the Evolution of Human Speech*. New York: Macmillan. *127*

Logan, F. A. (1969) The negative incentive value of punishment. In B. A. Campbell and R. M. Church (eds) *Punishment and Aversive Behavior*. New York: Appleton-Century-Crofts. *71*

Lorenz, K. (1966) *On Aggression*. London: Methuen. *75*

Lovaas, I. O. and Simmons, J. Q. (1969) Manipulation of self-destruction in three retarded children. *Journal of Applied Behavior Analysis 2*: 143–57. *79, 87*

Lovaas, I. O., Schaeffer, B. and Simmons, J. Q. (1965) Building social behaviour in autistic children by use of electric shock. *Journal of Experimental Research in Personality 11*: 99–109. *79*

Luria, A. R. (1961) *The Role of Speech in the Regulation of Normal and Abnormal Behaviour*. Oxford: Pergamon. *40*

Lutzker, J. R. and Sherman, J. A. (1974) Producing generative sentence usage by imitation and reinforcement procedures. *Journal of Applied Behavior Analysis 7*: 447–60. *60*

*Mackintosh, N. J. (1974) *The Psychology of Animal Learning*. London: Academic Press. *70, 106, 111, 112*

Maier, S. F., Seligman, M. E. P. and Solomon, R. L. (1969) Pavlovian fear conditioning and learned helplessness. In B. A. Campbell and R. M. Church (eds) *Punishment and Aversive Behavior*. New York: Appleton-Century-Crofts. *76*

Marler, P. (1970) A comparative approach to vocal learning. *Journal of Comparative and Physiological Psychology 71*: no. 2, part 2. *127*

Marks, I. M., Gelder, M. and Bancroft, J. (1970) Sexual deviants two years after electric aversion. *British Journal of Psychiatry 117*: 173–85. *42*

*Meyer, V. and Chesser, E. S. (1970) *Behaviour Therapy in Clinical Psychiatry*. London: Penguin. *29, 43, 62*

Miller, N. E. (1944) Experimental studies of conflict. In J. McV. Hunt (ed.) *Personality and the Behavior Disorders*. New York: Ronald Press. *71*

Miller, N. E. (1948) Studies of fear as an acquirable drive. *Journal of Experimental Psychology 38*: 89–101. *66*

Miller, N. E. and Dworkin, B. R. (1974) Visceral learning: recent difficulties with curarized rats and significant problems for human research. In P. A. Obrist, A. H. Black, J. Brener and L. V. Di Cara (eds) *Cardiovascular Psychophysiology*. Chicago: Aldine Press. *55*

Mischel, W. (1973) Toward a cognitive social learning reconceptualization of personality. *Psychological Review 80*: 252–83. *101*

Mishkin, M., Prockop, E. S. and Rosvold, H. E. (1962) One-trial object-discrimination learning in monkeys with frontal lesions. *Journal of Comparative and Physiological Psychology 55*: 178–81. *119*

Morris, D. (1968) *The Naked Ape*. London: Corgi. *90, 94*

Mowrer (1960) *Learning Theory and Behavior*. New York: John Wiley. *66*

Nicholson, J. N. and Gray, J. A. (1972) Peak shift, behavioural contrast and stimulus generalization as related to personality and development in children. *British Journal of Psychology 63*: 47–62. *106*

Nisbett, R. E. (1972) Hunger, obesity and the ventromedial hypothalamus. *Psychological Review 79*: 433–93. *92*

Parker, R. K. and Rugel, R. P. (1973) The conditioning and reversal of reward value. *Child Development 44*: 666–9. *96*

Paul, G. L. (1969) Outcome of systematic desensitization II. In C. M. Franks (ed.) *Behavior Therapy: Appraisal and Status*. London: McGraw Hill. *30*

*Pavlov, I. P. (1927) *Conditioned Reflexes*. New York: Dover. *11, 12, 18, 33–45, 73, 74*

Pliskoff, S. S., Wright, J. E. and Hawkins, I. D. (1965) Brain stimulation as a reinforcer: intermittent schedules. *Journal of the Experimental Analysis of Behavior 8*: 75–88. *91*

Premack, D. (1965) Reinforcement theory. In D. Levine (ed.) *Nebraska Symposium on Motivation*. University of Nebraska Press. *95*

Premack, D. (1970) A functional analysis of language. *Journal of the Experimental Analysis of Behavior 14*: 107–25. *128*

Premack, D. (1972) Two problems in cognition: symbolization, and from icon to phoneme. In T. Alloway, L. Krames and Pl. Pliner (eds) *Communication and Affect*. London: Academic Press. *131*

Pryor, K. W., Haag, R. and O'Reilly, J. (1969) The creative porpoise: training for novel behaviour. *Journal of the Experimental Analysis of Behavior 12*: 653–61. *58*

Purtle, R. B. (1973) Peak shift: a review. *Psychological Bulletin 80*: 408–21. *105*

Rachman, S. and Hodgson, R. J. (1968) Experimentally induced sexual fetishism: replication and development. *Psychological Records 18*: 25–7. *42*

Ray, B. A. (1969) Selective attention: the effects of combining stimuli which control incompatible behaviour. *Journal of the Experimental Analysis of Behavior 12*: 539–50. *110*

Reynolds, G. S. (1961) Attention in the pigeon. *Journal of the Experimental Analysis of Behavior 4*: 203–8. *110*

*Reynolds, G. S. (1968) *A Primer in Operant Conditioning*. Illinois: Scott, Foresman. *82*

Rogers, C. R. (1951) *Client-Centered Therapy*. Boston: Houghton-Mifflin. *62*

Rumbaugh, D. M., Gill, T. V. and von Glaserfeld, E. L. (1973) Reading and sentence completion by a chimpanzee. *Science 182*: 731–3. *129*

Russell, B. (1940) *An Inquiry into Meaning and Truth*. London: George Allen and Unwin. *124*

Sechenov, I. M. (1863) *Reflexes of the Brain*. See Boring, E. G. (2nd edn 1950) *A History of Experimental Psychology*. New York: Appleton-Century-Crofts. *9, 10, 12, 13, 18, 19, 117*

Seligman, M. E. P. (1970) On the generality of the laws of learning. *Psychological Review 77*: 406–18. *93*

Shepp, B. E. and Schrier, A. M. (1969) Consecutive intradimensional and extradimensional shifts in monkeys. *Journal of Comparative and Physiological Psychology 67*: 199–203. *112*

Sidman, M. (1953) Avoidance conditioning with brief shock and no exteroceptive warning signal. *Science 118*: 157–8. *67*

Skinner, B. F. (1938) *The Behavior of Organisms*. New York: Appleton-Century-Crofts. *17, 53, 106*

Skinner, B. F. (1953) *Science and Human Behavior*. New York: Macmillan. *47, 69, 87*

Skinner, B. F. (1957) *Verbal Behavior*. New York: Appleton-Century-Crofts. *117, 124–5*

Skinner, B. F. (1971) *Beyond Freedom and Dignity*. London: Jonathan Cape. *10, 17, 18, 19*

Skinner, B. F. (1974) *About Behaviorism*. London: Jonathan Cape. *17, 18, 19*

Slotnick, B. M. and Katz, H. M. (1974) Olfactory learning-set formation in rats. *Science 185*: 796–8. *112*

Sokolov, Y. N. (1963) *Perception and the Conditioned Reflex*. London: Pergamon. *24–5, 109*

Solomon, R. L. and Wynne, L. C. (1953) Traumatic avoidance learning: the outcomes of several extinction procedures with dogs. *Psychological Monograph 67*: 4, no. 354. *66–7*

Stein, L. (1969) Chemistry of purposive behavior. In J. T. Tapp (ed.) *Reinforcement and Behavior*. London: Academic Press. *90*

Stevens-Long. J., and Rasmussen, M. (1974) The acquisition of simple and compound sentence structure in an autistic child. *Journal of Applied Behavior Analysis 7*: 473–9. *60*

Stokes, T. F., Baer, D. M. and Jackson, R. L. (1974) Programming the generalization of a greeting response in four retarded children. *Journal of Applied Behavior Analysis 7*: 599–610. *51*

Stubbs, D. A. (1971) Second-order schedules and the problem of conditioned reinforcement. *Journal of the Experimental Analysis of Behavior 16*: 289–314. *99*

Sutherland, N. S. (1968) Outlines of a theory of visual pattern recognition in animals and man. *Proceedings of the Royal Society B 171*: 297–317. *120*

*Sutherland, N. S. and Mackintosh, N. J. (1971) *Mechanisms of Animal Discrimination Learning*. New York: Academic Press. *109, 110, 111*

Sutherland, N. S. and Williams, C. (1969) Discrimination of checkerboard patterns by rats. *Quarterly Journal of Experimental Psychology 21*: 77–84. *120*

Terrace, H. S. (1966) Stimulus control. In W. K. Honig (ed.) *Operant Behavior*. New York: Appleton-Century-Crofts. *106*

Thorndike, E. L. (1898) Animal intelligence. *Psychological Monograph 2*: no. 8. (Reprinted by Macmillan, New York in 1911.) *14, 17–18, 64, 69*

Tolman, E. C. (1932) *Purposive Behavior in Animals and Men*. New York: Appleton-Century-Crofts. *16, 57, 121*

Tolman, E. C. and Honzik, C. H. (1930) Introduction and removal of reward and maze performance in rats. *University of California Psychology Publications 4*: 257–75. *16*

Treisman, A. M. (1969) Strategies and models of selective attention. *Psychological Review 76*: 282–99. *111*

Truax, C. B. (1966) Reinforcement and non-reinforcement in Rogerian psychotherapy. *Journal of Abnormal and Social Psychology 71*: 1–9. *62*

Turner, L. H. and Solomon, R. L. (1962) Human traumatic avoidance learning. *Psychological Monograph 76*: 40. *66*

Valenstein, E. S., Cox, V. C. and Kakolewski, J. W. (1970) Re-examination of the role of the hypothalamus in motivation. *Psychological Review 77*: 16–31. *92*

Wahler, R. G. (1969) Oppositional children: a quest for parental reinforcement control. *Journal of Applied Behavior Analysis 2*: 159–70. *78, 87*

Watson, J. B. (1913) Psychology as the behaviourist views it. *Psychological Review 20*: 158–77. *13, 14*

Watson, J. B. and Rayner, R. (1920) Conditioned emotional reactions. *Journal of Experimental Psychology 3*: 1–14. *43*

Weiss, T. M. (1971) Effects of coping behaviour in different warning signal conditions on stress pathology in rats. *Journal of Comparative and Physiological Psychology 77*: 1–13. *75*

Wolf, M. M., Risley, T. and Mees, H. (1964) Application of operant conditioning procedures to the behaviour problems of an autistic child. *Behaviour Research and Therapy 1*: 305–12. *77*

Wright, A. A. and Cumming, W. W. (1971) Colour-naming functions for the pigeon. *Journal of the Experimental Analysis of Behaviour 15*: 7–18. *119*

Yule, W., Berger, M. and Howlin, P. (1974) Language deficit and behaviour modification. In N. O'Connor (ed.) *Language, Cognitive Deficits and Retardation*. London: Butterworth. *126*

Zimmerman, B. J. and Rosenthal, T. L. (1974) Observational learning of rule-governed behaviour by children. *Psychological Bulletin 81*: 29–42. *123, 127*

Subject Index

142